THE COLDSTREAMER AND THE CANARY:

LETTERS, MEMORIES AND FRIENDS OF ROGER MORTIMER,

PRISONER OF WAR No. 481, 1940 – 1945

edited by

Jane Torday

First published in 1995
by Black Cat Press, Nilston Rigg, Langley, Hexham, Northumberland NE47 5LD.

© Jane Torday 1995
ISBN 0 9525309 4 5

Typeset by Northern Writers Advisory Services, 77 Marford Crescent, Sale, Cheshire M33 4DN.

Printed by Birkenhead Press, 1-3 Grove Road, Rock Ferry, Birkenhead, Merseyside L42 3XS.

All rights reserved. No part of this book may be reproduced by any means without the written permission of the publisher.

CONTENTS

	Page
Introduction	1
Memories and Friends	7
Leading Up To War	10
War	14
Adjusting to Prison at Spangenburg (Oflag XI A/H)	27
The Canary Bird	42
Punishment at Thorn (Stalag XX A)	50
The Mud of Warburg (Oflag VI B)	59
Prison as a Way of Life at Eichstatt (Oflag VII B)	82
The Closing Months	132
The Darkness before the Dawn at Moosberg (Stalag VII A)	158
Aftermath	166
A New Beginning	172
Some Biographical Details	174
Index	178

LIST OF ILLUSTRATIONS

PHOTOGRAPHS

	Page
1. My father, Roger Mortimer, in his Coldstream Guards uniform, pre-war.	Front Cover
2. Roger and a fellow officer by Damascus Gate, Jerusalem, October 1938.	11
3. My father's sister Joan (1927).	22
4. The gates of Spangenburg Castle.	28
5. A bearded Roger.	30
6. John Surtees.	33
7. Fred and Ruth Corfield on their wedding day in 1945.	45
8. Roger 3rd from left, bottom row, and Jack 4th from left.	94
9. Jack Poole 5th from left, bottom row, and Roger 6th from left.	95
10. My father on the day he married my mother in 1947.	99
11. Anthony Bamfylde top row, centre and Francis Reed top row, right.	115
12. Roger Mortimer's friends.	116
13. Roger Mortimer's friends.	117
14. Desmond Parkinson.	134
15. On the left Martin Gilliat and on the right Freddie Burnaby-Atkins after the war, in New Delhi.	154
16. My parents on their Wedding Day.	171
17. The Mortimer family in 1965.	173

CARTOONS

'Stooges' at work. By Gordon Horner.	47
Christmas Parade. By Gordon Horner.	70
Card Game. By Gordon Horner.	92
"Surely not Sauerkraut in Christmas pudding, Old boy." By Gordon Horner.	125
"I say, can you tell me where one collects food – I'm a new Kriegie." By Gordon Horner.	141

DOCUMENTS

Freddie Burnaby-Atkin's Prison Identification Card, 1940.	143
My Father's 'Liberation' letter.	162

MAPS

POW Camps for Allied Prisoners.	56-57

"The experience of war in youth is indelible and awesome, though it can appear to be forgotten for decades at a time. At an age when one is just beginning to take on life on one's own account, a sense of the whole vast range of it is suddenly glimpsed in many startling aspects, including its remorseless indifference to the fate of the individual human being.

It is in this way that those who have been through a war are divided from those who have not: the most impressive thing in their life can seem already to have happened. This is why there is some compulsion to reach across the divide and communicate it."

(A Crowd is not Company by Robert Kee)

INTRODUCTION

If my father had written his autobiography – as I had often begged him to do – I would have been deprived of the solace, the pleasure and the interest of producing this memoir, which covers perhaps the strangest five years of Roger's life; those which he spent as a Prisoner of War in Germany.

In fact, Roger did start to write his own story some years ago, but within weeks, two people, quite unconnected with each other, whom he had written about in the opening chapters, died. This rather depressed him. He said he felt it might be some kind of jinx and abandoned the project forthwith. Actually, I don't think he wanted to write about himself. He genuinely thought it would not be very interesting. But even setting aside my bias as his daughter, I am confident that those who knew him either personally, or through his writing, would disagree. He was a fascinating and a complex character.

The job of racing journalist suggests a rather glamorous life, but the thing I mainly remember about it, as a child, was how hard he worked. Home was also his office, so he was there for much of the time, but it had to be respected that he was around but not necessarily available. He would be at his desk in the morning, then quite often at around midday, Peter Willet, fellow racing writer, neighbour and friend, would turn up and they would have a huge glass of sherry before setting off for the race meeting of the day. Then he often worked late into the evening, and as his study was opposite my bedroom, the clatter and ting of his old Remington typewriter was often the lullaby to which I fell asleep.

He enjoyed family life, and when he had the time to relax, he was one of the funniest of fathers, who could turn the most minor event into a good story and dazzle his audience with tales both probable and completely improbable. He was a great player of family fire-side games with us as children and could invest even a game of dominoes with a sense of high drama and humour. He loved devising general knowledge quizzes for us, which included such diverse questions as "What date was the Battle of Trafalgar?" and "What is the name of the fat black cat with a wart on its nose who lives next door?" He offered "Huge prizes, many riches for the winner", which was probably half a crown (12½p) but we all came away with something.

At the same time, he had an inhibition about people "making exhibitions of themselves" – wouldn't play Charades, hated T.V. quiz programmes which involved people doing absurd things to win a washing machine, and wouldn't come to see us in any event at school! Just occasionally, he would completely let his hair down, as when he once performed, unforgettably, his own interpretation of *Swan Lake*, all six foot of him, in the drawing room at home.

Readers of Roger's articles, books or letters will know that he was not only an amusing writer, but a highly literate and totally professional one. Not all those who found their way on to the printed page through his pen enjoyed the experience, as he never flinched from pricking the balloons of pomposity when he encountered them. He was a great debunker of anything he considered bogus or pretentious, and the adolescent phases of his children (a period when it is almost obligatory to dress strangely and develop controversial attitudes and opinions, something made absolutely inevitable in the case of my brother, my sister, and myself, being "children of the sixties") was made even less comfortable by heavy teasing, providing more amusement for any audience present than for the victims! I still have my father's letters to me from that period, and while some still seem masterpieces of biting parental wit, others show a kindness, concern and understanding of the trials and tribulations of youth that I didn't fully appreciate at the time.

Roger was very widely read and enjoyed discussing books and ideas; buying the most recent publications in hardback was the one personal luxury he regularly allowed himself. He was as likely to be reading a contemporary novel by a female writer – Anita Brookner, Penelope Lively, before they achieved eminence – as he was to be immersed in Dickens, Balzac or Tolstoy, a distinguished biography, or great tome of military or political history. Most of all, he liked to be amused. He adored Evelyn Waugh and thought *Decline and Fall* one of the funniest books ever written; I don't know how many times he must have read it. Being a very fast reader, there was always time to re-read great favourites. I rarely saw him read a racing book – but that was work. He felt that there were far too many books published of a repetitive, dull and mundane nature. He was very critical of slovenly and ungrammatical writing in literature and journalism.

It is clear that I am taking something of a risk writing in honour of my father. In the face of his very high standards, how do I dare presume to such a task? So it is probably best that I say now that I do not aspire to be in the same league as Roger. I have tried to tell his story simply, and if I have been tempted to swim out of my depth in places, I have tried to resist it. Two pieces of advice that he was fond of pronouncing have surfaced in my mind quite often while writing about him. The first, "My Dear Child, try to temper your hilarity with a modicum of decorum." The second, and rather contrary, Mortimer aphorism, "It doesn't matter how much balls you talk as long as you know you're talking balls."

There are a number of reasons why I wanted to compile this book, but my major motivation was my sustained interest in my father's war years, and the pride I felt for his endurance and courage as one of the first prisoners to be taken in the last war, who remained "inside" until the end.

About ten years ago, my father gave me an old envelope full of his POW letters. Of course he knew they would interest me, but he didn't want me to do anything with them while he was alive. He told me I could do what I liked with them after his death.

Although he had strong opinions on many things, my father was in fact a very modest person, with little vanity or personal ambition. He achieved a high place in his profession, but that was not through strategic manoeuvring or manipulating of other people – quite often the very opposite – he was just very good at what he did. He would be embarrassed and annoyed with me if I were to over-estimate or exaggerate any of his qualities, but his very nature – one of courage, honour, intelligence and humour, but not saintly, self-sacrificial or in any way self-satisfied – makes that impossible.

True to form, one of my father's sayings was "no one is irreplaceable". It gave him a mischievous pleasure to say it, but he knew it wasn't true, and at the end of his life, my mother more than proved that to him. It was as if the love-affair they had started forty four years previously had gone full circle, through all the vicissitudes of marriage, and ended at the point where it started.

My father – unique, inimitable and Yes – irreplaceable. Here is a very small portion of his life that, at the time, must have often seemed the longest stretch of it – his role in World War II, a contribution which was never recognised by any official power, but is another strand to be woven into the fabric of its history. I hope his letters and the memories of his good friends will tell a story worth the telling to everyone who knew and loved him.

Jane Torday

MEMORIES AND FRIENDS

I have been very fortunate in receiving so much encouragement, interest, and information, from a number of Roger's POW friends; from my mother, Cynthia; from my father's sister, Joan; from my brother and sister, Charlie and Louise, their enthusiastic support; from my partner, Tommy, his kindness, humour and consistent understanding; from my sons, Piers and Nicholas, their interest, comments and helpful criticism.

Without all of their help, this slender memoir would instead have been merely a thin one. I am indebted to everyone concerned for their support and their unfailing responses to my requests.

Each contributor has added something of value, another piece and sometimes several pieces, of the jigsaw. There are almost certainly still some holes in the final result, but this is a personal book, and so I appeal to its readers for allowances to be made for any oversights, undersights, or omissions.

I would like to say a particular thank you to Sir Frederick Corfield on whose autobiography I depended enormously to piece together the story of the 'Canarybird'. His account was the lynchpin of my efforts. A special thank you, also, to Desmond Parkinson, for permitting me to use extracts from his revealing and remarkable diary covering the last months of the war. Biographical details of Fred, Desmond and other friends are at the end of the book.

I would also like to thank John Surtees, Francis Reed, Peter Black, Freddie Burnaby-Atkins, Raoul Lemprière Robin, William Purdue, Lord Gerald de Mauley, Les Allan and Graham King of the National Ex-Prisoner of War Association, Jill Groves of Northern Writers Advisory Services, and my loyal friend and ally, Lavinia Orde.

I had more or less completed the book when I decided it was time that I read Robert Kee's book on his wartime experiences as an RAF bomber pilot who was shot down, captured by the Germans, and was a POW for three and a half years.

He started to write the book almost as soon as the war ended, when his experiences were still vivid in his mind. *A Crowd is not Company* (Abacus) was published in 1947. What I have fumbled to say on the effects of being in a POW camp, he has said with moving eloquence. He had direct experience of something I only know of indirectly, with the added advantage of being a writer of considerable stature with a number of books to his credit, articles for *The Sunday Times, The Observer* and *The Spectator* and also television documentaries.

As he summarises various aspects of World War II prison camps so illuminatingly, I have taken the liberty of quoting from Mr Kee at various junctures, with his permission, c/o Rogers, Coleridge and White Ltd.

Other sources which I have found very helpful: *The Second World War* by Martin Gilbert; *Chronicle of the 20th Century*; *Private Words, Letters and Diaries from the Second World War* by Ronald Blythe; *Undiscovered Ends* by Jack Poole; illustrations from *For You the War is Over,* by Gordon Horner – the phrase 'for you the war is over' being the regular refrain of German guards to their prisoners; *Articles of War: The Spectator Book of World War II.*

Under the heading 'The War Elsewhere' I have written a resumé of the main events of the war during the period covered in each chapter. To try and convey a sense of actually living through the war, and being informed of the News as it happened, I have written these notes in the present tense.

LEADING UP TO WAR

From at least 1933 onwards, it was evident that the potential threat posed by Hitler and Nazism was very serious. But if throughout the 1930s Hitler was building up a militaristic and racist Germany ripe for war, Britain had but one longing – for an enduring peace. With a very British mixture of honourable intention and apathetic inaction, the omens of the perils to come were disregarded until it was too late.

A cynical onlooker at developments on the world stage in the late 1930s was my father, Roger Mortimer, who was serving as a regular soldier, an officer in the Coldstream Guards and a member of the British Peacekeeping Force in the Mandate of Palestine. There were tensions between the Arabs and the increasing number of Jews seeking refuge in Palestine. In consequence, the Arabs revolted against the British administration and the Coldstream Guards were sent to Palestine in October 1938 to alleviate the problem.

In later life, Roger looked back on those pre-war Palestine days as a young bachelor Guards officer, albeit one on a marginal income, with tremendous affection and nostalgia. His old cloth-bound album of black and white photographs of that period suggest a rather delightful existence; the sun shining down on cheerful, crisp-shirted young officers, relaxing at the watering holes of Jerusalem or Alexandria. But the small remaining bundle of letters home to his father, Pop,

2. *Roger and a fellow officer by Damascus Gate, Jerusalem, October 1938.*

rather puncture that romantic image.

Incidentally, on leaving school, my father had wanted to go up to University at Cambridge, but against Roger's wishes, my grandfather sent him to Military Academy at Sandhurst, to shape up and get organised! In fact, that is just what he did. It was a great success, and my grandfather was forgiven.

*

Unfortunately, none of these letters are dated, but a number of them contain observations pertinent to the gathering clouds of war:

> 1. "The more I see of the army on semi-active service, the more hopelessly inefficient they seem to be; Thank God there wasn't a war. Some of the Battalions out here are absolute jokes, like the Worcesters who have lost five trucks, several Lewis guns, shot up their own patrols and run like Hell whenever they meet an armed gang of more than one. Then there are the Kings Own who are nothing more than an armed gang themselves, and the Royal Scots who are absolute savages."
>
> 2. "I'm glad I'm not in England at present, there seems to be so much squabbling, wind and national hysteria about. It may be dull here, but we don't worry much about Europe and there are worse conditions to be in than mine."
>
> 3. "The British Constables here are of three sorts:
>
> (i) Extremely good ex-N.C.O.s and a large number of Irishmen. They are brave, efficient and liked by the Arabs and the Jews.

(ii) A huge batch of new men; a very mixed collection, at present not much use.

(iii) A few really sadistic bullies – rather like Hitler's nastier Storm troopers. They do an immense amount of harm and judging from the brazen way that they kick, punch and beat harmless old men, they have never been checked by their superiors.

We're all beginning to get rather browned off as we're given no clue as to our future except the knowledge that there's no leave going this year. However, an *Ugly World Crisis* seems to be brewing up so there's a chance we may get shoved off to Egypt to keep the Italians quiet. What a fairly bloody world it is at present and not the remotest sign of any improvement in the future."

Undeniably, the future did not bring improvement.

WAR

When Britain went to war with Germany in 1939, the mood was very different from that in 1914. There was widespread disillusion with the government's ineptitude, its lack of perception on the true nature of the monster it was confronting in the escalation of the crisis which precipitated the country into war. The country was ill-prepared and poorly equipped for war. It was only twenty years since the end of the First World War and its effects were still being felt, red and raw, by many who had prayed they would never see its like again.

Back in 1914, my father was five years old. Young though he was, being both sensitive and observant, he absorbed some sense of the grimness of the atmosphere. His father too, was away at the front for a part of that war. He was one of the more fortunate, surviving intact both mentally and physically. But Roger could remember, living in London at a time when mourning was still worn, how half the women of the city suddenly seemed to be dressed in black following the Battle of the Somme.

Later, in the early 1920s, Roger at his first Remembrance Sunday Service at Eton, looked up and saw even some of the most hardened school masters' grieving faces, in many cases with tears pouring down, overwhelmed at the memory of so very many of their pupils who had gone to their deaths.

Now, he and his generation were committed to further conflict. No one knew what shape this war would take nor how long it might last, but it was understood that it could be a war of a very different nature; not a war against the armed forces of another country, but a war against a force of evil that was armed.

However strongly people felt it their duty to fight for King and Country, their commitment could not shine with the wholehearted patriotism of the innocent and romantic quality of 1914. The sense of momentum generated by the declaration of war in September 1939 dwindled in the uncertain atmosphere and inactivity of the "phoney war", which lasted until the Spring of 1940.

By the early months of 1940, Captain Roger Mortimer, at thirty years of age, was with the 1st Battalion Coldstream Guards as part of the British Expeditionary Force in northern France. Three letters home, undated and without address (the addressing of letters was forbidden), survive from that time, each one in a distinctively different mood, and I would guess written from different places.

I know this was written in February 1940. How peaceful it all sounds. There's no sense of the preoccupations of war whatsoever, but perhaps there is an underlying feeling that Roger is treasuring up this gentle idyll in the knowledge that it must come to an end.

"My life here continues to be distinguished solely by the completeness of its rural quietude: my former

companion has moved on and though I miss the conversation, the joint attack on *The Times* crossword, and the general knowledge papers we set each other every night, I am very happy in complete solitude as long as the post arrives occasionally and I have something to read. By good fortune, I managed to get hold of Tolstoy's *War and Peace* which I'd always shied away from formerly: I enjoyed it more than anything I'd read for years and it kept me quiet for almost a week.

The best of this sort of existence is that one is able to do all sorts of things that in more normal times one would never think of doing – at any rate, I wouldn't. I have become rather a keen naturalist in a primitive sort of way and spend a good many afternoons watching birds, and I think I shall shortly be able to publish a small brochure dealing with the life and habits of the little owl in this part of France. Now that the thaw has set in, I'm going to buy a rod and do a little coarse fishing in the canal."

The letter was incomplete but the remaining paragraph fizzes with that wonderful, utterly uncompromising Mortimer asperity:

"I'm delighted that *Hore-Belisha was sacked. In my opinion, he was a self-advertising careerist, a liar, not over-scrupulous, and a sucker up to the vulgar press."

This next letter too, possibly written before the pre-

---

* Hore-Belisha, Minister of War

16

vious one, is from a soldier in waiting, and furthermore, from one feeling rather put out that a weekend trip to Paris had been aborted by an unexpected visit from 'Some dim old bore of a general'.

"My Dear Father,
Fine warm weather here with very sharp frosts every night. I wish there was a golf course near, as it's just the right time of year for that sort of thing. I only wish we could hop down to the New Zealand Club on Sunday and play a round and a half, no doubt exceedingly badly, with a large lunch thrown in between.

I had arranged to go to Paris last Sunday with Rupert Gerard and Tommy Gore-Brown, but at the very last moment on Saturday morning, just as we were setting off, some dim old bore of a general announced his intention of inspecting us at 11 am on Sunday. This was equally tiresome for the guardsmen, as on Saturday afternoons we hire three buses and take a trip to the nearest town. Consequently, they had no time left to get cleaned up and everything swabbed for this singularly ill-timed visit.

We duly paraded on Sunday, but after a tedious wait, a message came through to say he would be an hour and a half late; I suppose we should have expected this, but nevertheless our feelings towards the general were scarcely improved by this announcement. However, I felt it my duty to give him a civil reception, so I posted some drummers with French 'Cas de Chasses' on the balcony of the turret and when he emerged from his staff car, they blew a loud and highly original fanfare – the sort of thing that precedes the entry of Prince Charming in a provincial pantomime. He was visibly shaken, so I seized the initiative and had him well under control the whole time. He proved to be a dim, pleasant sort of Belisha general: he inspected the men 'standing easy' if you please, and asked them all well-meant but fairly silly questions, such as 'Does your family write to you often enough?' I think he was pleased with his visit and he was very complimentary afterwards.

Unfortunately, Rupert and Tommy go up to their Battalions today and we shall miss them a lot as they have helped to make this rather dreary existence quite fairly amusing during the last six weeks. We had a dinner party last night in their honour (but which they paid for!) and a good time was had by all.

We have a padre living with us which is a pretty fair bore as he is both obtuse and foolish. He's not a shit in any way, rather to the contrary; but he's appallingly ignorant and out of touch with reality to such an extent that he really shocks me. Also, he is apt to make rather sly, smutty remarks to show what a jolly, broadminded sport he really is. Love Roger."

My father's frequently irreverent attitudes towards those whom he felt were inappropriately placed in positions of authority, or who were unduly pompous, provided his friends and contemporaries with considerable amusement. As my father admits in the following letter, the amusement was not so great for those were 'the butt' of his wit.

In the last letter written before my father was sent into action, where the preoccupations of war are now unavoidable:

"My Dear Father,
I was detailed to come up here at four hours notice from the Base. I was rather relieved in a way at not going to the 2nd Battalion where my memories are not of the happiest; moreover, the Commanding Officer used to be R.'s right hand man, and I'm afraid I never treated him with the respect due to his seniority, and spent a good deal of time and ingenuity in making him 'the butt'. The fact that we have not had to meet in the tenser atmosphere of war is a matter of mutual relief and if I'd been in his place, I should have been very loathe to receive me into his fold.

I'm a fairly junior captain in this Battalion and I'm doing duty as 2nd in Command to Jerry Fielden, which suits me well, especially as I have a Hell of a lot to learn about this sort of soldiering. Jack Whitaker is our Brigadier I'm glad to say, as no one could be nicer. Our C.O., Arnold Cazenove, is almost unknown to me; he is very serious, painstaking and industrious and demands (rightly, I think) a very high standard indeed. Anyway, I bet there isn't a better Battalion in the B.E.F. especially as regards turn-out; we work like blacks, digging every day from dawn until dusk, with occasional variations in the shape of 15 mile marches. I find myself very tired when my last duty is done, and more inclined for sleep than anything else.

I had a bloody journey up, taking 48 hours with two minor train accidents. I arrived at 4 p.m., very tired and dirty with the worst cold I've ever had, and shivering in a tremendous blizzard. At 8 p.m. we did a night drive: yours truly sitting in an open lorry with no windscreen, and then proceeded to walk back some sixteen miles, getting in at dawn. I felt like death when I started but 100% better at the

end.
Could you please send another issue of kippers, and a cake from Mrs. Tanner would be welcome. Our billets are easily the best in the BEF: we have a very good company mess, central heating, good W.C. etc. I sleep in the next door house, a very classy mansion owned by a rich industrialist. I have a delightful bedroom and get ragged a good deal by the seven children, who I frequently see sitting in a long row on *jerrys.
Best love to Mummy and I'll write when I get time. Am unlikely to get leave before the end of June."

My father didn't get leave in June. Instead, in the week following Hitler's invasion of the Low Countries on 10th May 1940, and two weeks before Dunkirk, Roger was wounded and captured while commanding his company in action on the Louvain Canal in Belgium. As one of the first prisoners of the Second World War, he was not to see his home or family again for another five years.

The initial news, however, was far worse. In the confusion of events, my father was reported killed. One of the first to hear was Roger's great friend (later my godfather), Raoul Leprière-Robin, Intelligence Officer of the 2nd Battalion – Coldstream Guards. He learnt this inaccurate information quite by chance, from Major

---

* Chamber pots

Jerry Fielden (to whom Roger had been second in command), while standing in discussion at a crossroads in northern France, a few days after Roger had been captured.

Not long afterwards, at the Mortimer family's London house, in Cadogan Square, Roger's sister Joan returned home after her first day as a WRN in uniform.

"It was about tea-time, and I found Pop opening a letter in the hall. It was from the Coldstream Guards to say that Roger had been killed – they should never have sent it. Pop said would I stay with him, so Posie Guinness from opposite went to fetch Ma in a taxi – she was cooking at the Victoria Station canteen. I remember Cousin Tom coming round, and a notice was put in *The Times* before we received, with relief, the glad tidings that he had been taken prisoner."

Over in Ireland, in the little Catholic church in the village of Grange Con, County Wicklow, candles were lit for Roger. It was a place very dear to his heart as he had spent so many happy holidays there with a favourite aunt, Star Mitchell and her husband Chris. Roger was not a religious man, but he was very touched when, later, he learned of this Christian gesture on his behalf.

Later in 1940, an article appeared in *The Times* on the Coldstream contribution to fighting action in May, in which my father was commended:

"When the enemy broke through on the Belgian front and brought fire to bear on the rear, another company held their positions on the canal, thanks to the inspiring leadership of Captain Mortimer, who was knocked unconscious and captured."

3. *My father's sister Joan (1927).*

Captivity marked the end of a civilised existence and the beginning of a chain of deprivations. In Roger's case, he was given, for the space of one night, a brief and unexpected respite from this fate. Between his capture in Belgium and subsequent transportation to a Prisoner of War camp in Germany, my father found himself the recipient of a rather unlikely invitation; he was summoned to dine with a German officer of high rank.

Before the war, Roger had met a German general on several occasions when racing at Ascot. The general was apparently fascinated by English flat racing and was interested to meet and talk to my father, who had already acquired a broad knowledge of the subject.

As one of those strange coincidences that occur in life, the general was based in Belgium at the time of my father's capture, and going through a list of British prisoners, he saw my father's name. He immediately made arrangements for my father to be brought round to his residence. A staff car, driven by a young German officer, arrived at the POWs' temporary base and picked Roger up. Allegedly, the officer was unable to read the map ... the sort of incompetence that would have delighted my father ... and Roger had to read it for him and guide him to the general's commandeered house.

The general welcomed Roger warmly and showed him up to a bedroom where clean clothes had been laid out for him. After the general had left my father to change, and gone downstairs, Captain Mortimer felt it was his duty to examine the general's bedroom in case there was anything of military importance there. All he found were beautifully ironed shirts and pyjamas embroidered with the general's initials on the breast pocket.

The general gave Roger a very good dinner, over which they discussed the war in a civilised fashion.

The next morning, after a good breakfast, the staff car reappeared, and the general said, "I'm afraid you will have to go back now." He added regretfully, "I'm awfully sorry about all this – I'd far rather be at Ascot."

Roger, once again in his rather dirty uniform, after this strange but diverting encounter with a German general, was returned to the other prisoners. From then on, his encounters would be with less entertaining Germans – camp commandants and guards.

1940: The War Elsewhere

May: Britain withdraws from Norway. Churchill replaces Chamberlain as Prime Minister. Hitler invades Holland and Belgium and pushes through to France. Churchill tells the House of Commons: "You ask what is our policy? I will say. It is to wage war, by sea, land and air, with all our might and with all the strength that God can give us; to wage war against a monstrous tyranny, never surpassed in the dark, lamentable catalogue of human crime. That is our policy."

June: The mass evacuation of British troops from Dunkirk. Churchill tells the nation "We shall defend our island, whatever the cost may be, we shall fight on the beaches, we shall fight on the landing grounds, we shall fight in the fields and in the streets, we shall fight in the hills: we shall never surrender."

Italy declares war on France and Britain. Paris falls to the Germans. Poland, Norway, Denmark, Holland, Belgium and France are now under German occupation. The French government sign an Armistice with the Germans at Compeigne, leaving two-thirds of France occupied. General de Gaulle, Under Secretary for War, declares, "Whatever happens – the flame of French resistance must not go out and it will not go out."

July: In France's unoccupied zone, at Vichy, Marshall Petain is head of the government responsible for the administration of the French Colonial Empire. The Royal Navy destroy a substantial part of the French fleet in Algeria to prevent it falling into German hands.

August: The Battle of Britain begins. It is calculated that 1,000 German planes are being sent over Britain daily. In a speech honouring RAF pilots, cheered throughout in the House of Commons, Churchill says, "Never in the field of human conflict was so much owed by so many to so few."

September: Italian troops advance into Egypt from Libya. The Blitz begins. Hitler plans and then postpones "Operation Sea Lion", the invasion of Britain.

October: The beginning of the Battle of the Atlantic and the terror of the U boats. German and Italian troops invade Rumania. Italian forces invade Greece from occupied Albania.

November: The worst single air raid of the war so far – the bombing of Coventry. (A new word enters the German language – 'Koventieren', to coventrate, meaning to annihilate or raze to the ground.) Britain retaliates by bombing Hamburg.

December: In the Western desert, the British make their first offensive against the Italians and capture the camp at Sidi Barani. The City of London is bombed and 20,000 firemen work to extinguish the fires.

ADJUSTING TO PRISON AT SPANGENBURG (Oflag XI A/H)

"You adjusted yourself to prison life. Unnatural conditions became natural and as time passed it was more and more difficult to believe that there was any other life beyond that which went on inside the wire. Certainly it was an adjustment which you fought against. it was claustrophobic to feel that the outside world, which reason told you was still there, was in fact disappearing. But adjustment went on all the same because it was the only way of making yourself tolerate a condition which you loathed. So the outside world faded."

(*A Crowd is not Company* by Robert Kee)

Spangenburg Castle in Westphalia was Roger's initiation into prison life. There are no remaining letters describing those first months of imprisonment, as far as I know. When Roger spoke of that time – not often – he always expressed the view that the first six months as a prisoner were in many ways the worst; adapting to the conditions of captivity, living with the uncertainty of events, coping with the discomfort of having virtually only the clothes you stood up in, and tearing the tail of your shirt to use as a handkerchief.

These were chaotic times. No one knew exactly what was happening and worse, what was going to happen next. There were no parcels of comforts coming through from home, or the Red Cross, on an organised basis yet. This disorder characterised PQW camps both in the first year of the war and in the final stages.

4. The gates of Spangenburg Castle.

Then there was the frustration, the depression, the sheer boredom of not only being disconnected from events, but also completely uninformed about them. Prisoners of War had no regular access to British news, save what they learnt from time to time from new arrivals. The only press news available to them came in the dubious form of glowing accounts of German victories in German newspapers.

There was little for even the most sanguine or optimistic of prisoners to pin their hopes on in these circumstances – save the only belief that sustains any prisoner in any war, that sooner or later, this war must end.

They were not accommodated at Spangenburg Castle for very long, but it was there that Roger met Fred Corfield (then a young regular soldier; later farmer, barrister, Conservative M.P. and subsequently Minister) who became not only a very good friend but also – as will be revealed shortly – a partner in a dangerous activity which dominated a part of every day of my father's term in prison, for four years, and made a vital contribution to prison camp life.

> Fred remembers, "My only clear memory of our stay at Spangenburg Castle was that Roger and I both grew beards, which, despite the expert attention of a bearded naval officer, we both found uncomfortable and later abandoned. We also endeavoured to produce a passable smoke from the rapidly fading leaves of Virginia creeper which covered the castle walls. It was not a success."

In September 1940, they were moved down to the Lower Prison Camp in Spangenburg.

Another friend who came into Roger's life at Spangenburg was John Surtees. From the most inauspicious beginnings, developed a friendship in which they remained in more or less monthly contact with each other

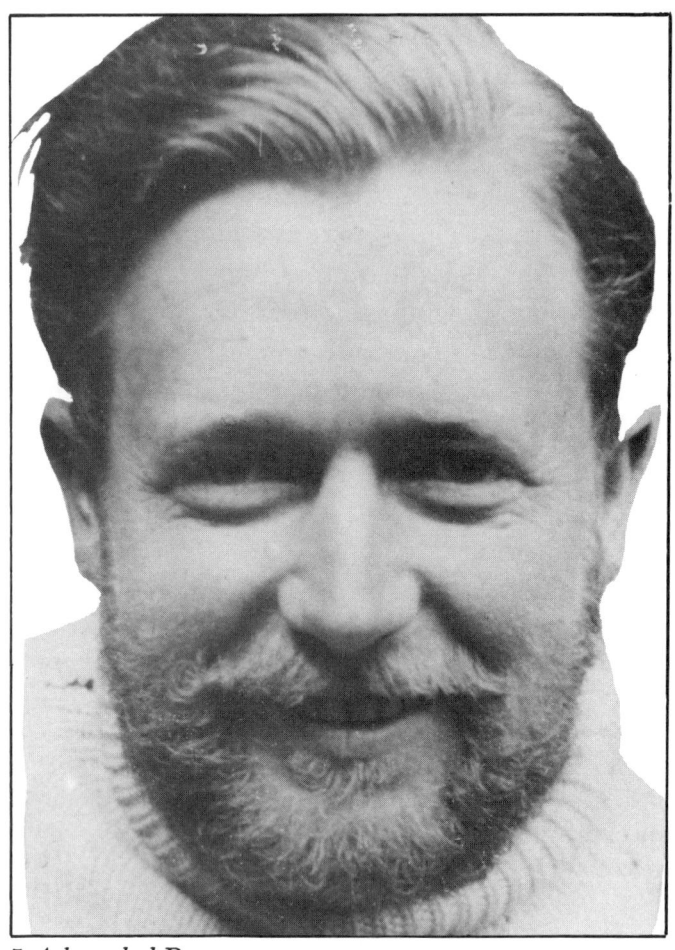

5. *A bearded Roger.*

for the next fifty years. Sometimes they wrote to each other 'Dear 481' (Roger's prison number) 'from 1204' (John's number). But this is how it was at the beginning, or perhaps at the beginning of the beginning:

"My first sight of Roger was at Corps Camp at Tweesledown in July 1935, when we young Etonian cadets struggled onto Parade in front of the tall, fair-haired, moustached and immaculate Guards Officer Mortimer, under whose temporary command fell the Eton College Officer Training Corps contingent. We were not smart, and it was not long before we became aware of it. Those who collapsed in the sweltering heat, some of them suffering from a hangover, had their names taken without delay by the Sergeant Major, on the orders of the Adjutant. No one was seriously penalised, but we regarded this officer with a certain amount of opprobrium, or at least, disfavour.

Five years later, in the autumn of 1940, on my arrival at Schloss Spangenburg from a French Hospital, there was the tall, fair-haired, moustached, luxuriantly bearded and now far from immaculate figure, dressed in a pale sweater and battledress trousers. He was dispensing a plate of lettuce sandwiches to members of our two dozen party. It was my bad luck not to be awarded a sandwich – an oversight which Roger was not allowed to forget for the next fifty years. It was the last sight of lettuce I had until 1945. We had been travelling by barge and cattle truck (40 hommes, 8 chevaux) for 14 days, counting the overnight stops, and we were famished.

Much later on I discovered that I had been disqualified because of my dress – French khaki knee breeches and a blue pullover certainly didn't indicate an army officer – 'Just possibly the RAF,' Roger had commented later, 'or even a Frenchman'."

Spangenburg had a mixed population of British Naval, Army and RAF officers, and Frenchmen. This little story seems to demonstrate that whatever general cameraderie might have oiled the wheels of prison life, there were times – as when food was very tightly rationed – when that cameraderie was rather selective. Members of the different forces of air, land and sea (and soldiers of different regiments), let alone those of another nationality, did regard each other with varying degrees of approval or suspicion.

The difference in age between my father and John was ten years – many of his POW comrades were considerably younger than him. But despite the lettuce sandwich, they made friends quite soon.

John and Roger were both old Etonians, which provided some immediate common ground. My father was always interested in Eton and I never heard him decry it; he sent my brother, Charlie, there, and was delighted when my two sons, Piers and Nicholas, got into the school. Yet remembering my father, John said that for the large part, Roger had been very unhappy at Eton, having been in

> "One of the most chaotic and indisciplined houses of the 1920s, where bullying and sexual misbehaviour were commonplace, providing a daunting and thoroughly unsettling atmosphere for a boy in his early teens, who was in any case of a sensitive nature. He made few friends there who lasted into old age, but the memory remained distinct and distasteful, a scar which never quite healed."

6. John Surtees.

I include this here, because painful problems, however well they have been overcome, leave their mark. We always carry the baggage of our past with us. It is as much a part of us as the present, and the load may not necessarily be a light one. For all his humour, wit and sense of fun, the darker side of my father was one of introverted melancholy and quite a bitter cynicism, which may have been the result, in part, of the two forms of internment to which he had been subjected – one in an unhappy corner of a British public school, and the other now, as a Prisoner of War.

A great sense of humour is, of course, one of the best – if not *the* best – form of human survival kit. As John continued –

> "Roger was naturally gregarious, made friends easily, and liked an audience, particularly one susceptible to laughter. The martinet of 1935 was quite kind after all. He taught me piquet, a game at which he excelled. He was entirely devoid of pomposity, a great raconteur and conversationalist, who was especially interested in the unusual, the memorable, the peculiar, the deviant.
> "Quite often he bestowed a nickname which stuck. Some of the names were well-known to the bearer; for example, 'Hen-coop' for Hasleden, a chicken farmer. A friend with size 13 shoes – Charlie Rome – became 'Boots', and Freddy Corfield, a farmer at heart, was soon allocated Dungy with a hard G."

A less jolly nickname was the one which Roger dubbed Airey Neave. Dungy Fred writes of the impression made by this fellow prisoner in 1940:

"Airey Neave had but recently passed his Bar exams and was so reluctant to forget it, that for this among other reasons, he was soon rechristened by Roger as: 'The seedy attorney' by which name he became almost universally known. Of course, we endlessly discussed escaping possibilities, but at that stage Airey was totally disinterested and rather tiresome. I remember him trying to organise a debating club and proposing the motion 'God is an egg', leaving the rest of us more than a little cold."

It should be added that in 1941, Fred describes Airey Neave in a far more complimentary light.

"He had by then become an almost entirely different person; he had lost his rather tiresome pomposity and entered fully into camp activities and plans for escape or otherwise making things difficult for the Germans."

Making things difficult for the Germans, provoking and teasing them, getting one up on Gerry, was of course one of the major diversions and entertainments of prison life. For obvious reasons, it was impossible for my father to recount any 'German baiting' anecdotes in letters home, and I wish like anything now that I had recorded some of the hilarious stories he told me when he was in the mood to remember these things. But in addition to 'Paul' my father was also nicknamed 'Gort', obviously rhyming with Mort, and also the name of the Commander-in-Chief of British Forces in France up until Dunkirk, Lord Field Marshall Gort! Anyway,

POW Gort is mentioned in the diary of a friend of Dungy Fred's, the late John Mansell, as getting into trouble for being cheeky to a German:

> "August 3rd 1940. Gort got into trouble. He had backchat with a sentry yesterday when gardening. The sentry had said to him, 'London will be entered in eight days.' Gort bet him something or other that it wouldn't be, and was arrested for bribing the sentries. The sentry, gesticulating, said that in six days Winston would be so high – bending down to illustrate the height. Gort pointed out that Hitler would be so high – bending even lower. The charge for this offence is 'insulting the Fuhrer'. Gort was given eight days confinement for his bribery and insults."

In fact, far from being a punishment, a short spell of solitary confinement was a relief. There were several occasions when Roger was chastised in this way and, in common with numerous other prisoners, he invariably regarded them as a pleasant respite from the incessant and intimate communality of POW living conditions – as long as he was accompanied by a book, if not several books.

I feel certain that Roger would have become a great reader whatever the circumstances of his upbringing, but losing himself in a good book was a pastime my father had cultivated during his relatively solitary London childhood.

Not unusually for boys of his background and generation, the person with whom he spent the most time, as a little boy, and to whom he turned for warmth and affection and in this case, humour and fun, was his Nanny, Mabel. When Roger was sent away to Prep. School (Wixenford, which became Ludgrove) – very often an objectionable experience in those days, but my father was as happy as anything to be in the country and in the company of other boys – Mabel's employment ceased. But he remained devoted to her and stayed in touch with her until she died, in her nineties.

When at home with his family, my grandfather, a sweet and gentle-natured man whose main ambition was for a peaceful existence, spent most of his time at his family firm of stockbrokers, 'Roger Mortimer and Co.', or on the golf course or in his London club. My grandmother's life was largely based on the values of the drawing room, from which she rarely strayed to the nursery or to Roger's bedroom to bid him goodnight or for any other excessive show of maternal affection. My father got on with his older sister, Joan, but she naturally had different interests and seemingly found more favour with her mother, to whom she was very loyal.

So, for my father, the ability to immerse himself in a book regardless of what was going on around him, always provided him with a comfortable refuge into which he could retreat wherever he was, whatever was happening.

Roger was not, of course, alone in this pleasure. Reading, for so many POWs, became the one way in which they could become free men and enter, through the printed page, any other world of their choosing. Ronald Blythe, in his anthology of wartime diaries and letters, wrote, "Stranded from the normal, taken for granted usefulness of their lives, people often felt that they would go mad if they could not occupy themselves in what was logical, rational and wholly personal. At a time when no one was left alone, there had to be an activity which required an aloneness that could not be criticised. During these years a book, for countless individuals, became the cell into which they could withdraw from the wearing enforced sociability the times demanded. Throughout the war, the call for books to be sent to ships, camps and prisoners grew ever more urgent as those who once may just have amused themselves with a tale or two now longed for that most effective escape from the boredom of their situation, the printed word."

As the war continued, postal communications became better organised and book parcels started to arrive in quantity, enabling POWs, if they wished, to study a variety of subjects. Many POWs were not regular soldiers, they had joined up as very young men, barely out of the schoolroom, and were therefore without qualifications for any occupation in peace. Some of them would have postponed or interrupted university in order to fight. Later, as the war dragged on, other soldiers, my father included, started to have doubts about the future of a career in the army. Their internment gave them, if nothing else, an opportunity to use prison as a kind of alternative university where they could bone up on anything from astronomy to the law, a subject in which Dungy Fred managed to qualify, as a POW in 1943.

It is slightly interesting to discover that the Germans could be quite obliging at supplying POWs with English classics published in Germany and apparently paid for out of POW monthly wages which came in the form of low value paper money known as 'Kriegy marks' (war marks). These had been arranged by some sort of international agreement on the basis that their small value would eventually be deducted from their army pay – a set-up which at one level seems surprisingly civilised for such uncivilised times and at another, perfectly outrageous that anything should be deducted from POW army pay. Fred Corfield's view, after the war, was that his reward was to have come through it all alive, and this small financial issue was not worthy of discussion.

Roger spoke a smattering of German and at Spangenburg, he endeavoured to teach Fred a little, "But Roger's sense of humour always got the better of him, and I only learnt the rudest words and expressions, which, being quite unrepeatable, I have consequently found of rather limited use."

Various German words crept into my father's vocabulary and remained there. If he wanted to cut short a discussion on an issue which he felt had been understood, and agreement reached, he would say with Teutonic succinctness – "Ja – stimmt". [Yes – Fine. O.K.] Mock horror or annoyance might bring forth a roar of

"Schwein!" or "Schweinhund!" But best of all was a kind of pot-pourri of German and army slang – "I'm going up to my zimmer to do a bit of Egyptian P.T. on my bracket." [I'm going up to my room for a sleep on my bed.]

*

There was little diversion from dreariness at Spangenburg. Roger decided to make a move to escape. Claiming to be suffering from appalling toothache, and acting up the part like mad, he was escorted out of camp to the local town dentist, who obligingly extracted a perfectly healthy tooth. After this slightly unpleasant experience, my father was permitted a moment's respite in the gents' lavatory. It was now his intention to make a getaway through the loo window. He did – only to be confronted by a German guard waiting patiently on the other side.

But these were early days and Spangenburg was only to be one of several prison camps. The autumn froze into winter, the first Christmas came and went. I have no record of it, nor what celebrations were improvised in prison, if any, then New Year and the beginning of 1941.

1941: The War Elsewhere

January: In East Africa, the British launch their attack against the Italians in Eritrea, Somaliland and Ethiopia. In North Africa, British troops capture Tobruk and Derna. The beginning of enemy air-raids on Malta.

February: Rommel's Afrika Corps land in Tripoli. British troops in North Africa take Benghazi. Bulgaria accepts German occupation. Hitler threatens a U boat war "of unprecedented fury" in the Atlantic.

THE CANARY BIRD

The first prison winter dragged drearily on, until one snowy, Sunday evening in February 1941, an event occurred which, as Fred described it, gave the POWs a lifeline which, "Short of victory and freedom, was virtual salvation".

This is the story. A small party of British doctors (who had been left behind in Belgium to tend the British wounded), were brought into the camp. Normally they would have been interrogated and searched before being allowed in. But it was a Sunday, and this precaution had been omitted, and the procedure was to be carried out within the camp.

Roger and Fred and about half a dozen others were housed in what had previously been a hayloft over the stables just inside the main gate. When the doctors came through the gate, they saw a group of prisoners nearby and as pointedly as they could, without attracting unwelcome German attention, they started gesticulating, pointing at a medical case which one of them was carrying, and indicating that they needed assistance.

Among Roger and Fred's room mates was Lance Pope, who spoke fluent German. He rushed to the gate and started distracting the guards by engaging them in conversation. Knowing the Germans' very apparent soft spot for children, he soon had them displaying their family photographs from their wallets, and avidly dis-

42

cussing their 'kinder' (children).

Meanwhile, the group of POWs, including Roger and Fred, had approached the doctors, and one of them surreptitiously handed over his medical case to them. They hurried it up to their room and opened it. Inside, in a mahogany case about ten inches long by four inches wide, was a four valve radio set: a very small object, but one which all those present immediately realised had a potential power totally disproportionate to its size – the ability to bring the voice of home directly into the camp and make the BBC news available to hundreds of prisoners of war.

> "Our first obvious step," said Fred, "was to reduce it to the smallest possible size, so we removed and destroyed its rather smart mahogany casing, to find it powered by four valves. By the grace of God it worked off German voltage, and its flex was fitted with the necessary adaptor to fit into a light socket; there were, of course, no power points available. Immensely excited, we tuned into the BBC and I shall never forget that first reception."

So 'the Canary bird' as the wireless became known, sang its first song that February Sunday evening in Spangenburg – "The Deepest Shelter in Town". It must have been a strangely stirring moment.

> "But the next imperative was to find a hiding place; floorboards were carefully loosened and lifted, and as luck would have it, our wireless fitted snuggly between

the joists among the remnants of the hay that had once occupied our loft."

Then they received the very first British news bulletin they had heard for months;

> "from which it was immediately apparent that the German papers had grossly under-estimated their own aircraft losses and correspondingly exaggerated ours."

They also heard the good news of Wavell's important victory in North Africa.

The British doctor responsible for bringing the radio into the camp had not wanted to keep it in his possession. There were undoubtedly very serious risks attached to owning an object capable of transmitting regular enemy information to a great number of prisoners. The doctor received payment for it, the story goes, to the tune of 460 marks.

A syndicate was formed to purchase the Canary and its new owners included Roger, Fred and John Surtees.

> Fred continued, "Whether Roger and I immediately took charge or whether we were elected to do so, I do not remember, and from then on, we took it in turns to take down the news virtually every night, only missing out when the radio was in transit from one camp to another. Although we each developed a personal shorthand, we were immensely helped by the marvellously clear diction of the newscasters, Alvar Liddell and the others. Of course Churchill's speeches were a gift, and enormously boosted morale.

7. Fred and Ruth Corfield on their wedding day in 1945.

Our drill was to write up our notes and summon a news conference of representatives from each room or hut, depending upon the layout of the particular camp we were in; the newscasters were sworn to secrecy and to return their notes for us to burn."

John Surtees didn't mention the improvised shorthand involved when he described the news relay system:

"Roger passed on a verbal bulletin to a posse of seven or eight sub-announcers, who each then relayed the verbal precis to the 100 – 150 officers in his own barrack block, or hut. A watchdog, or "stooge" kept a careful lookout for approaching Germans, and when necessary, gave a pre-arranged signal with hand or handkerchief."

For our prisoners of war, the arrival of the Canary and news broadcasts helped to get the world in perspective again, and offered them hope. It raised morale hugely throughout the camp.

But this boost was shortlived. About three weeks later, it was announced that the entire camp was to be moved to Poland in reprisal for what the Germans considered to be the unfavourable conditions in which their prisoners were being held in a POW camp in Canada, at an old colonial fort, Fort Kingston:

"But what the Germans had evidently failed to appreciate was that just before the outbreak of war, the Cana-

By Gordon Horner. 'Stooges' at work. Their jobs included guarding the Canary and keeping watch for its news team; keeping a watch out for German 'stooges', sometimes disguised as civilian manual workers in the camp; disposing of earth from escape tunnels.

dians had carried out a complete refurbishment and modernisation of the fort, at the cost of several million pounds – in those days a very large sum indeed. The result was accommodation of, at least by POW standards, very considerable comfort. However, the Germans resolved to retaliate and we were to be moved to a series of totally unmodernised forts in Poland," Fred recalled.

The Canary radio syndicate was immediately confronted with the problem of how to move their precious lifeline to Poland with them, without discovery. Fred wrote:

"We and our meagre belongings were always searched both on departure from one camp and arrival at the next. Although I always swore that I would never give details of either our packing arrangements or hiding places lest in some future war they be of value to an enemy – as so many first [world] war escape accounts were known to our captors (they always adorned the shelves of camp security officers – invariably SS – who clearly studied them), but the later introduction of transistors and miniaturisation has rendered our strategems no longer applicable."

Before leaving Spangenburg, "modest gifts" from the Red Cross had started to arrive and these included "medicine balls" – large, leather-covered, rugger-shaped balls measuring about fifteen inches by two foot. One of the men in the camp had previously been a saddler in a Gunner regiment in India. He skilfully unstitched a medicine ball, removed enough stuffing for the Canary to be securely concealed, sewn in, and travel undetected to Poland.

1941: The War Elsewhere

March: Rommel attacks British Forces in North Africa.

April: Rommel is victorious in Libya, and the British are besieged at Tobruk. Yugoslavia is invaded by the Germans. The British forces evacuate Greece. The Germans march into Athens.

May: The Germans invade Crete. 1,400 people are killed in the biggest single air-raid on London so far. In the Atlantic, H.M.S. *Hood* is sunk by the *Bismarck*. A few days later, the *Bismarck* is destroyed and sunk by British warships.

PUNISHMENT AT THORN (Stalag XX A)

"The journey to Poland was horrible – hundreds of miles in overcrowded cattle-trucks with occasional halts to relieve nature – and culminating in a march from the railway station to a peculiarly unattractive fort at Thorn. I (Fred Corfield) and my room mates, including Roger and a few other friends, managed to stick together. On arrival, we were conducted through stone corridors dripping with water, to a similarly stone-walled and stone-floored barrack of a room, almost as damp. Some more senior officers actually found the floor of their room – if such it could be called – submerged under several inches of water. The prospect was such that our only reaction was to laugh. That completely non-plussed the Germans, who could not make up their minds whether the British as a race were totally mad, or whether we were just being insubordinately defiant."

It was at this incommodious fort at Thorn that my father used to wake up with his blanket frozen to the wall, from the combination of damp and freezing temperatures. The ration of blankets was one per man. The food was of an equally thin quantity.

The POWs were 'under punishment' and the additional discomforts of Thorn, or in Polish, Torun, were fully intended. The camp, consisting of several forts was a Stalag, No. XXa. That was the category of camp for soldiers of other ranks – stalags. Oflags were reserved for officers and were supposed to observe the rules of the Geneva Convention laid down for those of officer status. The use of officers for forced labour was forbidden. Not so in the Stalags, where life could be very tough indeed. At worst, they could be Hell holes. It is a deeply regrettable fact that there was little to protect the imprisoned men from our fighting forces from being subjected to the most callous treatment.

Another old friend, Francis Reed, who first met Roger at Thorn, managed, despite its spartan conditions, to find something good to say for this camp.

"Thorn was a small camp and although physically uncomfortable, seemed to have a happier atmosphere than many other camps – perhaps due in some measure to the excellent Senior British Officer, Brigadier Nigel Somerset. Another important factor was that for the first time, we were able to receive the British news."

For some, parcels were getting through, with warm clothing, but not, I anxiously read, for my father, in this postcard to his cousins, Tom and John Blackwell – the first POW communication home from Roger that I have in my possession:

31st March 1941. 36 Gepruft, Stalag XXA.

"I think you'd laugh yourself sick if you saw my new home. Dartmoor Castle simply isn't in it. I've never lived below ground level before, but you soon get used to it. The weather is the worst part – bloody cold and still snowing. My winter clothing parcel has never arrived and I've had no news from my family for over three months as they won't write by Air Mail. Have opened the cricket season and find I'm really rather good with a rubber ball. Roger."

I find it hard not to feel a small sense of daughterly outrage for Roger that these ordinary but crucial comforts – not only warm clothes, but affection and news from home, were not arriving. I don't know why Air Mail was not used; I can only guess that either it was the constant risk of planes being shot down, or the expense.

The next card to Cousin Tom is written in a wistful mood but with the ironic humour that is associated with Roger. The turnip was not Roger's favourite vegetable...

April 16th 1941.

"My Dear Tom, this letter may be a trifle incoherent as I'm feeling rather sleepy after a truly delightful lunch of turnip stew – you can imagine how pleased I am to get so much of my favourite vegetable. I heard today that Snake-Hip Johnson had handed in the dinner pail; I only hope the *Cafe de Paris didn't go with him. Most of all I miss a comfortable WC, *The Sporting Life*, women and music. I've been trying to learn Russian but my enthusiasm is

---

* The bombing of the Café de Paris in which the Jazz musician, Snake-Hip Johnson, was killed.

dwindling and I think I prefer lying on my bed reading of past years' racing and thinking of bygone, happier days. I still do PT every morning, as then my conscience permits me to do damn all for the rest of the day."

As was common in prison camps, the beds were in the form of double bunks (sometimes triple) and they were almost the only places where, in this camp at least, people could relax, read during daylight, and kept reasonably dry.

"At Thorn, the Germans daily brought in British soldiers from a neighbouring camp for other ranks, and it soon became apparent that the other ranks' camps were very less closely guarded than ours, so several officers were very soon making plans to change places with any of the soldiers coming into the fort who were willing to do so."

Airey Neave was one such officer but although he successfully got out of the camp, he was soon recaptured. He was briefly returned to Thorn, full of praise for the Poles who had helped him, before being dispatched to *Colditz, considered to be virtually an es-

---

* Colditz is the prison that invariably jumps to mind when German POW camps are mentioned – consequently my father has sometimes been described in the press as a Colditz POW, which he was not. Writing to my godfather

cape-proof fortress, but from which Airey Neave successfully escaped. Tragically, destiny had another end in store for him; as a Conservative Minister in Mrs. Thatcher's government, he was ear-marked by the IRA and killed by one of their bombs.

Meanwhile, despite the primitive conditions at Thorn, the operators of the Canary Bird managed to keep everyone informed of the latest news, from which they learnt that:

> strains in the agreement between Germany and Russia were becoming increasingly evident. Eventually we began to be aware of substantial German troop movements in our own area; some were apparent from the little we could see of the surrounding country from our somewhat inadequate fortress windows."[*]

Peter Black in the 1980s, Roger always updated him on any ex-POWs he had news of. "I see Mike Edwards and his wife from time to time – I like them both – He went to Colditz and likes exploding all the bullshit written about that place." 'Krieg' being German for war, long term POWs were known as 'Kriegies'. Roger also wrote to Peter – "I'm looking forward to John Surtees's 70th Birthday fiesta at the Grocer's Hall. I expect quite a lot of crumbling ex-Kriegies will be there."

[*] All statements in quote marks without accompanying explanation are taken from Fred Corfield's autobiography.

Further information was provided by the daily intake of British soldiers.

"By this time, we had identified a German officer who was clearly a gentleman and certainly no Nazi. He confirmed our impression of a substantial build-up of German forces, and obviously disapproved of our accommodation.

Ultimately, the Germans recognised that a lot of British prisoners, within what was likely to become a war zone, might have disadvantages to themselves, as well as to us. At the very short notice of only a day or two, we accordingly set off on our travels."

1941: The War Elsewhere ...

June: Hitler invades U.S.S.R. Italian troops surrender in Abyssinia.

July: The US and British government freeze all Japanese assets; Japan retaliates by freezing all British and US assets. Japanese troops advance into Cambodia and Thailand. Britain and USSR conclude a mutual assistance pact.

August: Defending their country, Soviet troops pursue Stalin's "scorched earth" policy, destroying everything that could assist the enemy – they blow up the massive Luin Dujeproges dam. In Paris, 5,000 Jews are rounded up for deportation. Roosevelt and Churchill issue join declaration of war aims, the Atlantic Charter.

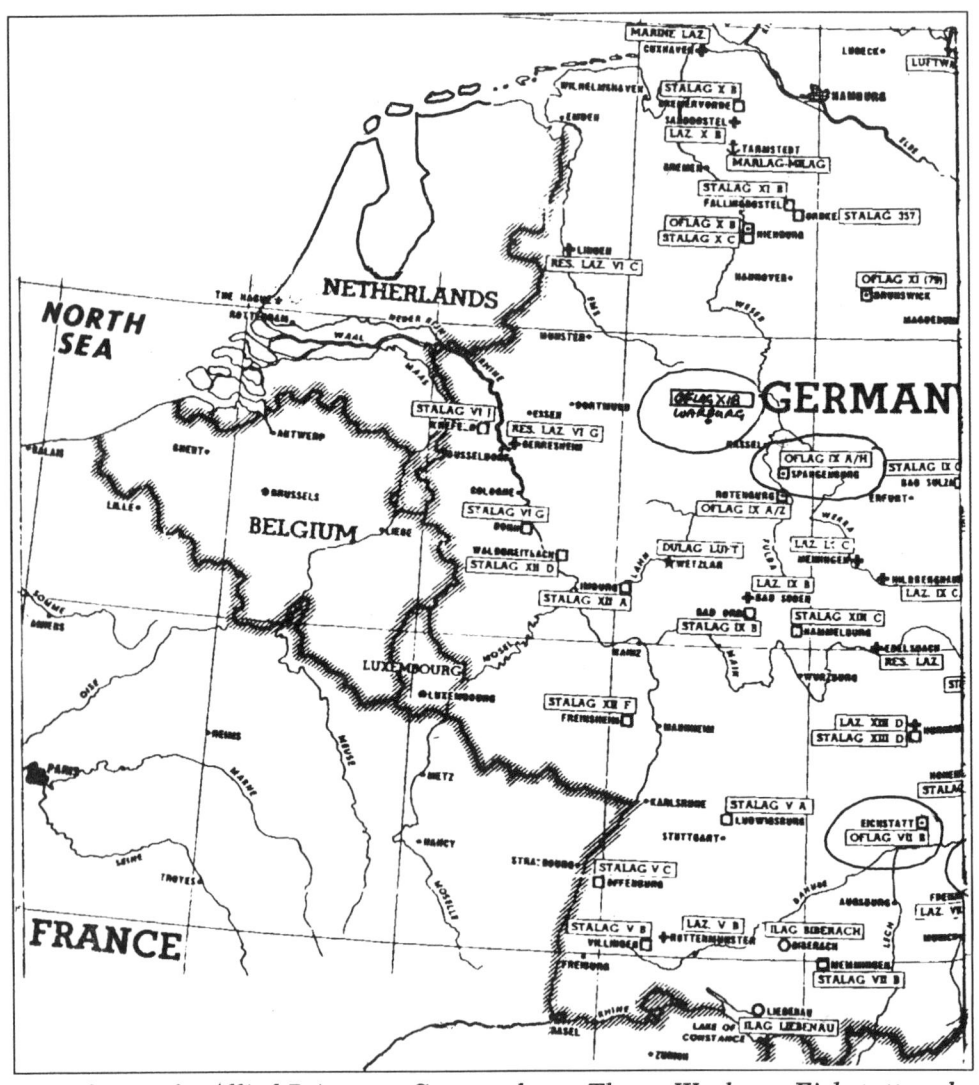

POW Camps for Allied Prisoners. Spangenburg, Thorn, Warburg, Eichstatt and

Moosberg are all marked.

September: The Battle of Leningrad rages throughout the month. All Jews in Europe are ordered to wear the Star of David and are forbidden to leave their living areas without permission.

October: The Battle of Leningrad continues. Moscow is under siege. In Japan, pro Axis General Tojo is appointed war minister.

November: The *Ark Royal* aircraft carrier is destroyed by U boats. The 8th Army, the 'Desert Rats' break through to make contact with the besieged garrison at Tobruk. Malta suffers its thousandth air-raid.

December: The Japanese bomb Pearl Harbour. America is now at war. Britain declares war on Japan. The Japanese invade Malaya and land on the Philippines. The British battleship, the *Prince of Wales* and the battle cruiser *Repulse* are sunk by the Japanese. Hong Kong falls to the Japanese. In Russia, harsh winter conditions are helping to reverse the fortunes of the Germans.

THE MUD OF WARBURG
(Oflag VI B/2 Bn)

Returning to Spangenburg after the rigours of Thorn, the former camp must have seemed a relatively desirable habitat. In August 1941, Roger wrote home quite cheerfully, mentioning a whole list of "regular correspondents" from whom he had received lots of letters.

> "I'm very well and have taken up running: I'm a bit old for it and my attempt to equal *Jimmy Langley's record run over the same distance failed. However, I'm going to train harder and mean to improve."

The Canary Bird too, was safely back at Spangenburg, having travelled in its medicine ball. As regards its transportation, John Surtees said:

> "A large measure of responsibility fell on the shoulders of Private Goldman, a camp orderly of non-Aryan parentage and with a noticably strong dislike of the Germans. Until the summer of 1941, a small sub-committee from our room had managed the Canary. At about that date, a more senior committee, which was set up under the Senior British Officer to co-ordinate escape plans, took control of the operation of the machine and the distribution of news. Roger and Fred remained its principal operators. A wireless expert was co-opted for

---

* A fellow Coldstream Guards officer.

wireless maintenance. On two or three occasions, a worn out valve needed replacement; this was achieved by bribery of, and subsequent pressure upon, a suitably compromised German guard. The softening-up process had to be repeated at intervals as the contingents guarding us were moved on to other places and replaced."

*

I wonder whether Roger's initial enthusiasm for gardening was first kindled in prison camp? The pleasure of managing to produce a few flowers at least, a splash of colour and beauty in those barren places. At all events, gardening became one of my father's great pleasures – it was a marvellous antidote to writing. His long herbaceous border in the garden of my childhood home, Barclay House in Yateley, Hampshire, blazed with summer colour, and he took great pride in his handsome display of dahlias; he was very keen on bedding plants, and the borders at the front of the house were regularly changed – summer snapdragons and lobelia following the tulips and forget-me-nots of spring. Roger also gained huge satisfaction from spreading manure whenever and wherever possible – he was never happier than when trundling a large wheelbarrow brimming with what he described as a "really rich and steaming mixture". We children had few reservations about being pushed along for wheelbarrow rides in the same vehicle afterwards.

A letter to his father, September 18th, 1941:

"I'm afraid I must be a dreadful nuisance to you but all your efforts are certainly appreciated at this end. The Red + too is settling down and we get one parcel a week from them at present. The garden has rather a bedraggled look at the moment, but our roses are quite nice, particularly 'Betty Uprichard' and 'Crimson Glory'. Sunflowers and pumpkins are also successful. I'm having a small party here tomorrow in my new room, which has a most lovely view and is easily the best I've had – very quiet and only two others in it, both old friends. Did I tell you there is a friend of Sophie's here? Philip Moore, minus a leg, and one of the nicest people you could meet anywhere. His leg is off at the thigh but has healed well. He does the most astonishing high jumps, well over four feet. Could you send a possible book or two on racehorse breeding and if possible, also some gramaphone records. We're settling down now for the winter and I feel sure that another two Christmases will see me home again. The worst of life here is its awful pettiness, lack of privacy, and the fact that captivity brings out the worst in you. I'm really delighted I have no peace-time friends with me here: one really sees so much of people that you suddenly find yourself hating people you know are really very nice. You've got to be pretty tolerant to be on term of more than honeymoon proximity with people for fifteen months, day in, day out, and not occasionally go off the deep end. Love Roger."

"The effect of overcrowding was the disastrous one of turning you against all humanity. Your mind became numbed to everything about human beings except that they pressed close around you all the time, that they slept above or below you, that you could never turn your head without seeing some evidence of their closeness – their clothes or books or their photographs – that they made it impossible for you ever to be alone. Although this was no fault of theirs you hated them for it."

(*A Crowd is not Company* by Robert Kee)

Unfortunately, my father's hope that he was settling down for the winter in his room with a view, was not to be. In October 1941 Roger, Fred, John Surtees, Francis Reed and others were moved to another part of Westphalia to a huge camp where it was the German intention to concentrate as many officers as possible.

This was Warburg, described by Francis Reed as a 'vast mud heap of a camp' consisting of endless huts situated on a high, unutterably desolate and very exposed area. The camp conformed to the bleak visions one has of such places – surrounded by high, double barbed-wire fences, about 12 feet high and with 6 feet between the inner and outer fence – the space between the two being filled with rolls of barbed wire. There were watch towers with search lights and armed guards every hundred yards or so.

Soon after arriving at Warburg, another set of huts enclosed by similar fencing, were erected immediately adjoining the main camp. This was to accommodate Russian POWs. It is well-known how appallingly badly treated Russian prisoners were, for a variety of reasons, and their conditions were not ameliorated by regular parcels from home – there were no such comforts available for them. When they arrived, they were in the most desperate physical condition, and initially they were brought into the main camp to be deloused. British POWs were allowed no contact with them, but realising that they had absolutely no 'kit', they thought it would be kind to provide them with some soap at least. They threw some over the heads of the escorting Germans. The Russians promptly seized it and started to eat it. It was learnt later that many Russian prisoners had died, and some were secreted under camp floorboards and in a few cases, ultimately eaten by their starving comrades.

*

Bridge had been played on the train journey to Warburg, which makes everything sound rather civilised. I don't know that it was. My father wrote to my grandfather in September:

> "Am settling down now in 2 Bn, VIB. It reminds me rather of Arrowe Park where I was in 1939. It was quite a long train journey here and we passed the time by playing a few simple games; our opponents at one moment went for a large slam with clubs, and I was unfortunately unable to stop them fulfilling the contract: luckily the results were not costly. I'm sorry there has been a gap in my letters but that

was unavoidable. Amongst my fellow prisoners are my hatter, Herbert Johnson, a most charming person, and a dreadful man who has for years pursued me with insurance policies. There is no escape now. There are far too many Scotsmen in this camp. They really are the world's dreariest race, the result I suppose, of a lifetime spent in damp, granite hovels in the Highlands. I've written to everyone I ought to, but of course safe arrival is not guaranteed. The snow arrived the same day as the Packe's boots, which made them doubly welcome. Give my very best love to Mummy, Joan and all at Norcott, not forgetting Plaice. I do hope his boy is still safe and sound. Love Roger."

I think my father was more prejudiced against the world in general at this point, than the *Scots* in particular. Although he clearly found those he had met dull, and, in his book, that was a far greater offence than many more reprehensible sins!

Escape was, of course, a constant preoccupation for most POWs. As a pastime, escaping was not of instinctive appeal to everybody and of course there were those who preferred a quiet life and did not wish to risk adding to their troubles or expending their energies on what so often proved to be fruitless enterprises. For many others, escape was a natural objective and a stimulating form of occupational therapy. There was a definite pressure on POWs, as it was British government policy that whenever reasonably practicable and possible, they should devote their energies to devising means of escape. Considerable ingenuity and courage was deployed in escape plans. But by the end of the war, of the thousands who had made the attempt, many managed to get out for a few hours or a few days before being recaptured, but only a small percentage, a few hundred POWs in Germany, had succeeded in crossing the border and getting home. But the endless plans that were laid, and the many brave attempts made, were not in vain. They kept the Enemy on their toes, and helped to distract them and disrupt their activities. John Surtees remembers:

> "On one occasion in 1941, Roger and I planned to escape together by substituting ourselves for 'other rank' members of a working party who went outside the camp to collect stores, coal, parcels, and so on. It never came off because our haversacks, which had been taken out and concealed in bushes by the co-operating men a day or so before, were discovered. We were threatened with reprisals to the whole camp if we didn't declare our identities. That earned us fourteen days each in solitary confinement; Roger regarded it as rather a peaceful alternative to camp routine," and John added, "But his cell had a better light for reading than mine did."

Roger did his fair share of tunnelling, and a new room mate at Warburg, and later a most beloved friend of my family, Desmond Parkinson, tells a story of tunnel failure. Tunnel digging, particularly using the primitive methods of the early days, was very far from being a fun activity, being both arduous and debilitating, and its collapse brought more relief than disappointment:

"Shortly after arrival at Warburg, Roger started a tunnel from the bath house and I was one of his slaves on this project. Others included John Surtees, Fitz Fletcher, Freddie Burnaby-Atkins, Michael Price. In those days, tunnelling techniques were very primitive and, as we had to dig a shaft sixteen feet deep before starting on the tunnel proper, fresh air at the working end was non-existent and I still remember the terrible headaches we all had after doing our stint at the face. But, as you can imagine, with Roger as our tunnel master, there were many light moments. But I don't think any of us had much faith that we would eventually emerge on the other side of the wire. This lack of faith was not misplaced, since after a heavy rainstorm, a senior (and to me, very elderly) major, decided that this was the moment to dig his little vegetable patch outside the bath house. This led, in short order, to the collapse and flooding of the tunnel and then the subsidence of the bath house itself. A pity after so much hard work, but I remember greeting the disaster with a big sigh of relief.

This did not deter our intrepid tunnel-master and we were soon at it again, starting from a room in one of the huts, but, perhaps more mercifully, our efforts were discovered by the Germans after a very short time indeed."

(As time went on, tunnel ventilation was slightly improved by making tubes from milk tins sent by the Canadian Red Cross, and driving the air through them to the workface with manually operated gramophones, which were also provided entirely thanks to the Red Cross.)

A Warburg wash house also played another role. As ever, one of the first priorities on arriving at a new camp was finding a safe hiding place for the trusty Canary. Fred describes the solution at Warburg:

> "For want of anything else, it had become almost universal practice to keep our washing kit in one of the boxes in which our Red Cross parcels were delivered. We therefore used one of these boxes for the wireless, which we hung beneath the seats covering the latrines, situated over a particularly noxious pit, in a hut four or five yards from one of the doors to our hut. Every morning and evening I marched to the wash house clutching my Red Cross box: in the evening I returned via the latrines and exchanged my washing box for the one containing the radio: in the mornings I repeated the action in reverse order."

Hot showers were only available once a week or so, but despite very cold weather and quite deep snow during the winter, Fred thought it would be a good self-discipline to take a cold shower every morning "thereby also creating a habit which would give me credibility should any officious German question the regularity of my wash house visits".

> "In some camps the lavatories were so bad that white slugs bred in the depths. You could see the filth heav-

ing with them as you peered through the crudely cut holes in the wood which served for seats, and sometimes they would crawl through these holes and invade the neighbouring parts of the camp. In other camps rats lived under the seats and bit people as they sat there naked. In others there was merely an overpowering smell when the wind blew in your direction. But it always seemed impossible that you would ever sit on the polished seat of a flushing lavatory again."

(*A Crowd is not Company* by Robert Kee)

Red Cross boxes were also used for conveying the spoil from any tunnel being constructed; it was then decanted into trouser pockets with a hole in which wearer's finger would be plugged until he had walked to a place where the spoil could be released down a trouser leg. The spoil was usually a completely different colour from the top ground of the camp, the pitfall that usually alerted the Germans to a tunnel project.

I am pretty certain it was in that freezing Warburg winter that Roger wrote home saying that he was cold, and could some corduroy trousers be sent to him? My Aunt Joan wrote to her great friend Ethel Cummins in America, and she sent him some trousers plus a wonderful, thick, duck-shooting coat. My aunt said:

> "Roger loved that coat – he said it saved his life. He came home in it at the end of the war and kept it for a long time afterwards. But the trousers met a slightly sad fate. Soon after he received them, he was summoned to the Commandant's office. The Germans pro-

duced a pair of shears and the legs were cut off the trousers and then stored away in a cupboard. Roger waited for a safe interval of time, then sneaked into the office, stole back the legs and wore them up his sleeves for extra warmth."

On November 14th, my father wrote home to my grandfather a letter that was, in effect, his 1941 Christmas card to about thirty different people:

"Best Christmas wishes to you, Mummy, Joan and all at *Norcott,[2] including **Plaice, Emily and the Staff. Same to Lily, Mrs. Tanner, Mabel and Nanny, Barrett, Thompson and above all, that very pretty maid with big blue eyes who was so wasted as a parlour maid. If you can remember, include Mr. Jauncey, the barber, Birks and Newark, and if you ever go to Lords, the tennis staff. With a bit of luck, I may be back next year, a bald, bent, toothless dyspeptic with a horrid temper scarcely improved by chain smoking strong French cigarettes. Actually, joking apart, I'm pretty well apart from a heavy cold and a broken rib sustained by mobbing about with a very amusing old Harovian publican, Edward Shape. Now for a few facts: many thanks for the clothes (what a nice, rather pansy sweater), all the chocolate, *Ruff's Guide*, *Nimrod Life*; I cannot always tell where V.S. (Voluntary Service)

---

* My Great Uncle Geoffrey's home near Berkhampstead, where my grandfather stayed for part of the war.
** The splendidly named butler at Norcott.

XMAS PARADE

By Gordon Horner.

parcels come from and I'm more than scared of appearing ungrateful, especially to Ethel, whose coat is the envy of the camp. Please thank Uncle for the books and Aunt Shirley for letters. Also *Sophie for a lovely libellous letter, Jane Nelson, Ralph Cobbold, Star, for letters. Could you sometime spare a second to ring up Peggy Dunne who has written marvellous letters every single week since I've been in chokey, as well as sending scores of books. Well, best love to you all; keep cheerful, never worry about me, even if you aren't getting letters, and keep the trap door of your siren suit buttoned up. Roger."

I don't think my father could have forgotten anybody in that letter. He was a most assiduous thanker; no one who made a gesture on his behalf ever went without acknowledgement. He wasn't insistent about much as a parent, but he was fanatical in impressing on us children the importance of thank-you letters. I'm afraid he didn't immediately succeed as I still have the regrettable evidence of letters he wrote to me in my teens, roundly chastising me on this account. As so often with the principles parents endeavour to instill in their children, I didn't fully appreciate the pleasure or the value of letter-writing until I was grown up. Nonetheless, I know I could never attain his prompt standards – if possible, Roger had written Christmas thank-you let-

---

* Lady Sophie Lyell.

ters by lunch time on Christmas Day! He had practically written the letter before the present was out of its wrapping paper.

*

Few people feel at their best in February, a month when it can feel as if winter will never end, that long grey lull between Christmas and Spring – a kind of seasonal depression which the dreariness of prison can only have magnified. Desmond Parkinson said cf Roger, "He was always gloriously pessimistic, but his gloomy views were well leavened with his own particular wit and humour." The following February (1942) letter to his father is a classic example – Roger's ironic wit keeps the underlying gloom at bay:

> "I'm afraid my letters are the last word in dullness but I am up against the same difficulties as yourself. I have had to give up skating as my knees wouldn't stand it and I could only progress rather unsteadily like a rabbit with a broken leg. Time fairly flies in prison and I can't believe it is over two years since I was last in England. One's occupations are very varied here: today, I'm room orderly, and have many menial duties to perform: in addition, I've had a German lesson and darned a three inch hole in my socks. I think I have only two ambitions in life left: to possess a water closet and to be able to hire someone to darn my socks. I hope you won't entirely give up golf as I intend to stage my first comeback against you at New Zealand (golf club).

With any luck I may have forgotten my previous style and will launch out with something new and hard enough to achieve any measure of success. I wonder which of us two will age most: if you keep your head and don't overdo things, you'll probably find yourself taken for my younger brother. I suppose there'll be a lot of nice, young, rich widows knocking about after the war. I only hope they won't all be sold out before I get back. Well, best love to you all. I am confident I shall be home within two more years. Roger."

In July 1942 he was more cheerful:

"Your letters come through extremely well now and seldom take more than three weeks. I received a very nice parcel from Mrs. J. last week, and I have one in store (I expect from Mrs. Miller) which I haven't drawn yet. I'm more grateful than I can say. Many thanks, too, for *Admiral Rous* from Uncle Geoff, a Lonsdale book from you, and two excellent agricultural books, I think from Aunt Shirley. I also got two books from an unknown source. Many thanks for these. I particularly enjoyed *Admiral Rous*. The weather here is perfect and I just lie about in the sun without any clothes on and let my mind go completely blank. The time passes admirably and I only emerge from a state of semi-coma at meal times. I played my first game of prison tennis last week – half an hour on a mud court, two balls, both wet and black, no stop netting at all. Prison life has several advantages. For the first time for twenty years I'm free from financial embarrassment; however many letters arrive, it's long odds against a bill. Secondly, even if I have to live at a very humble scale after the war, it can hardly fail to be a slight rise on my present condition. Also it's marvellous having no dreary routine: if I feel like it, I just go back to bed after breakfast and stay there till evening appel. Thank God I've always been bone idle and never felt the restless urge to do something. Love Roger."

Twenty years on from this letter, my father was paying school fees for three children and was doing more than the equivalent number of jobs; as racing correspondent for *The Sunday Times* (in pre-Murdoch days) racing commentator for the BBC, columnist for *The Racehorse*, and Public Relations Officer for the Horserace Totaliser Board which was the best paid job of the lot. Often a book on racing history was in progress, and there were freelance articles too. But it is true to say that Roger never looked for work. His ability and professionalism meant that work always sought him out.

*

Suggestions for plans of action for Prisoners of War started to come through, sometimes in the form of coded messages from the BBC. Another friend Roger made as a POW, Jack Poole, commented:

"The messages took hours to decode and were often of such a futile and trivial nature that they were not encouraged. I think one was to the effect that escaping officers should wear rubber-soled shoes, as they would then make less noise when walking through villages!"

News and information were also obtained from RAF pilots coming into camp after being shot down in Germany or Western Europe. Fred comments on a distressing coincidence which occurred as a result of one pilot's arrival:

"This RAF officer was insensitive enough to boast of his affair with a fellow officer's wife: the husband was among his audience."

One of the coded messages proposed that priority in escaping should be given to RAF officers or the more technical arms of the Army; sappers, gunners and signallers.

"Not surprisingly, this was highly unpopular with our 'Escaping Officer', who was an infantryman, and I do not remember whether he took much notice of this direction, which in any case have been difficult to follow — so much depended upon the enterprise, ingenuity and courage (often pretty foolhardy) of the individual. However, knowledge of this direction possibly exacerbated the 'problem' of Douglas Bader."

I cannot resist including Fred's observations on this extraordinary hero:

"Douglas was a quite astonishing character, brave as a lion, but also sometimes less than tactful and very obstinate. He was determined to escape, and used this fresh directive to substantiate his claim to priority, totally ignoring his disability. How he imagined he would either be able to walk any distance on his aluminium legs, or avoid immediate recognition if seen by any German over about five years old, has remained a mystery. He also enjoyed baiting the Germans, particularly when on roll-call parade, when he often had them beside themselves with rage; indeed, on more than one occasion he carried his teasing so far that had he not been physically restrained by his fellow prisoners, I am sure he would have got himself and the rest of us shot."

My godfather, Peter Black, described:

"A successful escape attempt from Warburg (August 1942), over the wire with scaling ladders. The electricity was shorted, or whatever the term is, and teams of people rushed to the wire with ladders and held them while the escapees scampered over and away into the countryside. Night-time, of course. Henry Coombe-Tenant in my regiment (Welsh Guards) got home from this escape. I think most were recaptured but it was a gallant attempt."

Fred was one of this brave group who managed to escape and breathe in the air of the outside world for about ten days, before being caught.

Meanwhile, Roger continued broadcasting operations with the Canary as usual, but August had not been an encouraging month for him. It is one in which he admits to some knowledge of the 'news'. He is at a low ebb in this letter to his father:

"There is a slight argument going on at present about letters for German officers in Australia, and in consequence I have not heard from you for some time, but I expect things will be straightened out soon. I have been having a ten day period of meditation which makes a change, and am soon to embark on another one. Delighted to hear John is alive but I'm sorry to hear of his accident. God knows, I know what Hell that sort of thing is. It will be terribly boring for him I'm afraid, but at any rate he is with friends. There is only one game to play during convalescence of that sort and even that brings more disappointment than pleasure very often. In some ways, it's not a very good thing to have close friends in the same ward, even the very nicest people's limitations become apparent when you see them all day and every day. The weather here has been rotten all summer and the news one long series of disappointments. I don't feel any nearer home than I did two years ago. However, it will happen one day, and although patience has never been one of my few virtues, I'm prepared to wait for this. I'm beginning, at last, to feel rather middle-aged. I read this in a book yesterday and I thought how true it was. 'The best one can hope for, once youth is past, is that age will blunt one's perceptions to the miseries of life.' Paul is having an unsatisfactory summer term at school, I hear. I'm afraid he does not get on very well with the masters. This letter is rather depressing, I'm afraid, but I've got a liver like a hob-nailed boot."

All the enforced intimacy of prison life meant that

one particular form of intimacy was rarely possible – sex with another person. Clearly that person could not in any case be a woman. There were none. But human beings have an infinite ability to adapt their needs to their circumstances. Those needs may be as much emotional as physical, and just as the British single sex boarding school system has inevitably encouraged intense liaisons between people of the same sex, so did the confinements of prison camp. There was a society of many young, attractive, virile men with not all that much to do. The living conditions of POWs probably kept young men's sexual urges more subdued than would have been the case had they been free, but at the same time, the very fact of men being caged together no doubt led to relationships which might not have occurred in a freer society. Prison more or less compelled celibacy on its inmates but that didn't completely eliminate love or lust and whether prisoners fantasised about their wife or girlfriend or lover, there was only one form of relief available. I am sure this is alluded to in the previous letter.

I have already mentioned that Roger was known by his nickname 'Paul' – after 'Pol Roger' champagne – to many Coldstream friends, and I'm sure that the Paul he refers to in the above letter, 'having a bad term at school and not getting on with the masters', is himself. Whether he is referring to the Germans – with whom he may not have been *persona grata* at the time of writing, or whether it refers to some senior officers, one of whom I have been told did not appreciate 'Paul' or his sometimes disrespectful and unsparing wit. Fred mentioned various officers, with a tendency to pomposity, whom Roger may have offended.

"Always a debunker of pomposity, Roger had, from time to time, included bits of purely local camp concern in his news bulletins. As these tended to be criticisms of some aspect of camp administration, they were not always popular with our seniors!"

In September 1942, Roger and others were transferred to another camp – this time to Eichstatt in Bavaria.

1942: The War Elsewhere

January: The Churchill/Roosevelt Declaration of the United Nations is signed by twenty-six nations opposed to the Axis powers. The Japanese take Manilla, land on Borneo, New Guinea, the Solomon Islands and Malaya.

February: The continuing escalation of the war in the Far East. A devastating setback is the Fall of Singapore, described by Churchill as "A heavy and far reaching defeat". The Japanese also invade Sumatra and Burma.

March: The RAF begin a round the clock bombing offensive on arms factories and German controlled industries in France. The Nazis begin the deportation of Jews to Auschwitz.

April: The Japanese take Bataan, in the largest scale American surrender ever, capturing tens of thousands of Allied prisoners. British Commandos, aided by the French Resistance, attack the big U boat base at St. Nazaire and inflict considerable damage, but many prisoners are taken by the Germans.

May: Bath, Exeter, Norwich and York are bombed. The RAF bomb Cologne in an attack four times the size of the worst air-raid on London. US and Filipino troops surrender to Japanese on Corregidor. The battle of the Coral Sea.

June: The Battle of the Midway. The US destroy Japanese battleships, warships and aircraft in the Pacific, in one of the biggest naval encounters in history. Rommel's troops take Tobruk and an estimated 25,000 prisoners are taken. In Egypt, the 8th Army abandons Mersa Matruh and the Germans take 6,000 prisoners. In the U.S.S.R., the Red Army launches an offensive on Sebastapol.

July: In Egypt, Auchinlek's forces beat back a great German desert offensive and hold the line at El Alamein. After a nine month siege, Sebastapol falls to the Germans. Twenty-nine ships out of a thirty-three strong Allied convoy are destroyed. Bomber Harris,

Chief of Bomber Command, gives a broadcast in German declaring the RAF will "scourge the Third Reich from end to end".

August: The Dieppe Raid, commanded by Mountbatten, is the biggest assault on Hitler's Europe so far, but is a costly failure. The losses of men and equipment on both sides are heavy. Over 1,500 Allied prisoners were taken. The Germans advance on Stalingrad.

PRISON AS A WAY OF LIFE AT EICHSTATT (Oflag VII B)

Eichstatt was a much more civilised camp than Warburg. Peter Black remembers:

"We were for the most part in what had been a proper barracks. There were some huts at one end of this camp, called 'The Garden City'. People used to exchange places and go there for a 'holiday'. You weren't supposed to change places and there was trouble if you were found out."

It was at Eichstatt that the Canary was temporarily silenced for the first time. If the news was very dispiriting, as it had been recently, this might have been a relief. John Surtees said:

"The news of two calamities – after the direst of winters at Warburg – the Fall of Tobruk, and then later in 1942, when we were sent to Eichstatt immediately after the failure of the raid on Dieppe planned by Mountbatten – made some of us wish we hadn't got a wireless. But, of course, it was a Godsend, even when the war was not going so well. As the tide eventually turned, news of such events as Stalingrad, El Alamein and the Normandy landings, gave an unimaginable injection of renewed hope for the end of the war. We knew the Germans knew we had the wireless. It is astonishing that they never found it, because they were constantly undertaking searches for it."

On arrival at the camp, the Germans decided to confine their 'search' of prisoners' belongings to personal kit, and sports equipment and other communal luggage were all locked in a store to be dealt with at some later date. In a way, this was just as well, as the much sewn seams of the medicine ball were becoming worn enough to arouse suspicion if it had come under close inspection. Fred had learnt lockpicking at Thorn, from an RAF officer. When the time was right, he picked the store lock and safely extracted the canary from the medicine ball, which was stitched up for the final time and now put into retirement.

After a few months at the camp, the original Canary was put into retirement as well, as Eichstatt and all other POW camps were supplied with more up-to-date and compact transistor radios. There is a possibility, I am told, that the original Canary is in the Imperial War Museum.

Neither Roger nor Fred wanted to keep the Canary in their block because another group of POWs were planning to start a tunnel just outside their room. But they found an attic in another block where the roof beams were so badly infected with woodworm that it was possible to hollow out the main beam to make a large enough space to conceal the Canary, and it is suggested that this attic became their broadcast reception centre at Eichstatt.

The transistor and other contraband, such as maps and compasses, arrived concealed in legitimate pieces of equipment supplied by the Licensed Victualler's Association. The new Eichstatt Canary arrived packed into the back of a darts-board.

On 19th September 1942, Roger wrote to my grandfather from Eichstatt:

> "I'm afraid you may not have heard from me for some time owing to us all moving camp. Most of us came on here but one of my oldest prison friends went off to a smaller camp, I think owing to the severity of his war wounds. The journey here was easily the most comfortable I've had in this country and we passed a very comfortable night in second class carriages. The surroundings of the new camp and adjacent town are remarkably pleasant and a striking contrast to the last place. The camp itself is also rather better and will probably be alright once we have organised it efficiently. Unfortunately, I am separated from several old friends as I'm living in a special block for those with a 'prison past'. However, I'm in a room with seventeen extremely nice people, most of whom I know well and with whom I've been messing for the past twenty-seven months. Still, these partings and breakings-up of old messes are rather sad things in prison, where one's whole existence and happiness depend on comradeship and living with people whose views and habits are roughly similar to one's own. However, I'm in a very pleasant mess with Freddie Corfield, Terence Prittie, Tony Rolt, Gerry Pilkington, John Cripps and Hector Christie. Tony Rolt is a well known motor racing man, and like most of the others, is a Green Jacket."

Later in September 1942, he sent a card to his mother in a slightly lower key:

"I'm in a new camp surrounded by very pleasant country. I'm not looking forward to my third gaol winter and hope to God there won't be many more. I don't think I have a single illusion left to shatter and my disgust for the entire human race is complete. That, actually isn't quite true. There are enough really nice people here to make life perfectly tolerable."

The majority of Roger's letters in my possession, were addressed to my grandfather, but always included a message of affection to my grandmother. As there were severe restrictions on letters, I don't know whether he wrote to her much individually, apart from the odd postcard like the one above. My grandmother spent part of the war staying with friends in the country, independently of my grandfather.

The output of POW letters home was limited to two per month, per prisoner. Letters were written on standard forms, five inches wide, printed with twenty-five lines, on which Roger usually fitted twelve words per line, in pencil – I don't know if ink was available.

The forms had basic information and the address printed in German. Whether they were camp issue or supplied by the Red Cross, I don't know. Each one was checked by the camp censor, who then put a huge sticker with his number on the back, e.g., 'EXAMINER 7464'. The postal date stamp was invariably two – three weeks after the date the letter was written. All incoming mail was censored as well. It wasn't possible to exchange views on the progress of the war let alone indicate any of the more interesting enterprises taking place in captivity.

My father wrote home just before Christmas 1942:

> "We are faced with a nasty domestic problem this morning as we are quite certain our cat committed a nuisance here last night, but we can't find traces of the crime. Cats are so apt to do these things in most improbable places. We are spending Christmas quietly – a large breakfast and then lying in bed until suppertime. Very many thanks for 360 Players cigarettes. I have a lot of Sept. and Oct. letters from you and Mummy. Please if you can, thank Joan, Aunt Shirley and Guy Stanford for kindly writing. I like to hear that D.L. is a Major: it doesn't make one feel the least bit of a dingy has-been. I told the news to someone in his regiment and he swooned quietly away. I'm reading as much history as I can and have just plugged gamely through 2,000 pages of Garven's *Life of Joe Chamberlain,* and am now cleaning up Palmerston, with Morley's *Life of Gladstone* as a little treat in store. The great thing about reading history is that it confirms my impression that human nature is not only nasty, but what is far worse, extremely foolish too. Prison is an amazingly good eye-opener on human nature, especially in the early days when things weren't too good. I'm playing in a knock-out bridge competition with Gerry Pilkington as my partner. The only fun is the amazing people you find yourself playing against. I'm thinking of taking an ecclesiastical

course next year: I believe the Church of England could be made into a very paying racket. Best Love to you all. Roger."

1942: The War Elsewhere

September: U boat attacks continue to worsen. Temporarily, the Germans chain up 2,500 Allied prisoners captured after the Dieppe raid, claiming it is in reprisal for the British chaining German prisoners. The Germans attack Stalingrad and are fiercely resisted; the battle develops on a scale unprecedented in this war.

October: The Battle of Stalingrad continues. The RAF carry out the biggest raid of the war on Italy, on Genoa. Montgomery leads the troops to victory at El Alamein.

November: Church bells ring out all over Britain, for the first time since 1940, rejoicing at the victory at Alamein. Rommel is in full retreat and thousands of Axis prisoners are taken. Of this decisive battle, Churchill said, "It is not the end. It is not even the beginning of the end. But perhaps it is the end of the beginning."

Tobruk is recaptured by the Allies. Hitler orders the reoccupation of Vichy France. To prevent the Germans utilising the French fleet at Toulon, the French destroy their own fleet, within hours of the arrival of German tanks. The captains of all the vessels stay on their bridges until the ships go down.

December: 107,000 US troops arrive to liberate Vichy French North Africa. In the first step in the campaign to free Burma, British troops advance down the Malayan peninsular. At a declaration read simultaneously by governments in Washington, London and Moscow, the Nazi slaughter of the Jews is condemned.

*

To ring the changes, in January, Roger swopped letter-writing places with a friend and room-mate, Hector Christie. Roger wrote to Hector's parents, and Hector to Roger's. If my father was able to confide the deep despondency he sometimes felt to his father, Hector's letter to my grandfather must have left him in no doubt that his son was playing a bad hand extremely well, with great humour and style.

Roger started the letter:

> "Well thank God 1942 is over. A drearier year I've never known. Many thanks for the cigarette parcels which have just arrived. You must be fantastically bored with my drab little bits of personal news, so this week Hector Christie will write to you and I am doing the same for him:"
>
> "This will probably be even more drab, but I thought perhaps you'd like to know that the old job is really well, in terrific form and confident, like me, that it will be any day now. The funny part of this is that I've absolutely no idea who I'm writing to, but I gather that I'm not likely have an infuriated and injured distant relative asking how I

dare describe the 'dear boy' as an 'old job'. Although we none of us are actually getting very much younger in age, some of us have gone a good way back mentally. I spent a most unpleasant night last night, with nightmares brought on by the combination of a very good dinner, quickly followed by a real mashing-up I was given, having just got into bed, from an incredible object wearing little but a shirt and a white sort of nightcap with a coloured bobble on the top, pulled well down over the ears, the whole being rather short of a shave, our combined ages being seventy, gives you some idea of a rather amazing display. However, it all passes the time and we manage to laugh a lot. Roger really is very well and has brought the art of living this life to a very fine point. I wish I could take things quite as easily and smoothly, although I find the good example of a morning in bed a most excellent one that suits me well. I really feel you will be seeing him this year, and you won't find, I think, that this dreary little time has done any harm whatsoever to a quite irrepressible person. Yours sincerely, Hector Christie."

Well, two army officers approaching middle age mobbing up in the dorm with bobbled nightcaps does present a slightly bizarre picture – but what the Hell! Laughter was the one tonic that was both free and available.

※

"Each man had his everyday business in which he could feel he had his niche and even at times his indispensability. Almost every condition of the outside world was reproduced in prison camp and provided the same outlets, fatuous and valuable, for human energy.

For the bureaucratic minded there was camp administration, and there were good and bad bureaucrats. For readers there were books and rooms set apart as libraries and there were people who learnt a great deal and there were people who read furiously and learnt nothing. For actors and producers and carpenters and for people who liked seeing plays there was an auditorium. For those who liked cleaning their buttons there was button polish and a British Parade once a year on the King's Birthday. For those who 'liked a job to do' there was the distribution of food and clothing and fuel, and there were some who did it honestly and others who were suspected of turning it into a 'racket'. For those who liked to go to church there were padres of several denominations and candles and a camp built altar. And for those who liked to go to the office every morning by 8.15 there were classrooms and classes where nobody learnt very much but where everybody thought they were doing something. Games players cleared areas of sand or dusty rubble. Strategists pinned up maps. Gardeners dug gardens. And people who liked to walk and talk walked round and round the perimeter track in endless identical circles.

As soon as prisoners had been poured into the particular patch of ground which was to be their camp, all this activity materialised from nothing; and it materialised in every camp regardless of the nationality of the prisoners. It was quite spontaneous, for the Germans instigated nothing, although they would sometimes co-operate in an elementary way by allow-

ing wood for goalposts or permitting the construction of a theatre. The ceaseless thrust and bustle came from something deep and primaeval in man. The restless indifferent force of human energy, responsible alike for beauty and ugliness, comedy and tragedy, saintliness and crime, had to find its own level inside the wire."
(A Crowd is not Company by Robert Kee)

*

A diversion that became almost an addiction for quite a number of POWs in Eichstatt in 1942, was gambling. Jack Poole described how he and Roger, and another, Bobby Gilroy, were appointed as chief stewards to oversee the gambling activities –

"A kind of Tattersall's Committee to attempt to regulate gambling to reasonable proportions and to enquire into any malpractices or disputes, and I am sorry to say that more than once we had to black list a cheat. One of the most common methods used by these slick gentlemen, when playing roulette, was to spot an inefficient croupier and then, with hand or elbow, move the stake on to the winning line, column or colour. Many of the swells played 'settlement after the war' rules, and in the majority of cases, this was strictly honoured. A few suffered from loss of memory, and one officer defaulted to a tune of nearly two thousand pounds."

A middle-aged schoolmaster found himself in debt to the tune of eighty pounds, which he was quite unable to

By Gordon Horner.

pay, but he honoured his debt by mending worn-out socks at the charge of five shillings a hole.

(Another responsibility of Roger's was working with the camp security team, and many years after the war,

Francis Reed heard of a British officer, who, suspected of treacherous dealing with the Germans, had been warned by a 'certain person' that he might meet with an untimely demise unless he mended his ways.)

In his letter to his father in February '43, Roger mentioned,

> "I'm a member of the camp Betting Control and Restriction Board; my co-member is Jack Poole, who is really a splendid person. He is older than the average – forty-eight – is always even-tempered and usually extremely amusing, and brings a welcome breath of *"Whites" into this place. He is in your old unit. We are also partners in a humbler sphere every day, i.e. at either end of a long saw on the wood dump."

Nice, kindly Jack, whom I remember coming to visit us as a child, died some time ago. He had the unenviable distinction of having been imprisoned in both the First and Second World Wars. In the First World War, he escaped from prison three times only to be recaptured; the fourth time, he safely crossed the border into Holland and freedom. In the Second World War, he made a break from a column of prisoners on the march, after the Battle of Calais, 1940. He acquired civilian clothes from a sympathetic French priest, and then buried not only his uniform, but his identification disc. He

---

* Whites Club, St. James's.

8. Roger 3rd from left, bottom row, and Jack 4th from left. Two rather contrasting snapshots of Roger and Jack, amongst others. In the first (No.8) the sun seems to be shining and they appear well and cheerful. The second picture (No.9 on p.95) is much more sombre. I wish I knew the history of these photographs.

was recaptured and having no identification disc, he was interrogated as a spy. After a few days, this possibility was discounted and he was sent to Laufen POW camp. But he observed:

> "Under the rules of war, the Germans would have been entitled to shoot me as a spy. In the turmoil after Calais, no names had been taken, only numbers. Consequently I had not been registered as a POW. Had the Germans been retreating or even static, this book

94

9. Jack Poole 5th from left, bottom row, and Roger 6th from left.

might never have been written," he wrote in his autobiography, *Undiscovered Ends*.

Fortunately the book was written, and Jack delighted me by saying that if he could have selected a cricket XI to take on any combination of German prison camp officers, he would have placed "Roger Mortimer behind the wicket, as he would let nothing go by".

Aside from Jack's double misfortune of two periods of wartime internment, perhaps neither his experiences, nor my father's, differed widely from those of countless other officers imprisoned by the Germans. But every individual interprets the trials that befall them according to their own lights, and the further time stretches away from those two wars, the more compelling personal accounts of those events seem to become. We are still tied into that period of history, we are still connected to it – but the sand trickles through the hour glass, and the time will come when we will not be able to hear of those overwhelming events, at first hand, from those who endured and survived them.

Those accounts of war which come not from admirals, field marshals or politicians, those who direct the action – but from the many others who were merely caught up in the events of their time – these are the stories which so often demonstrate a quietly heroic standard of human behaviour, certain unselfish values, and that extraordinary British sense of humour which never quite loses sight of the essential absurdity of things.

When Hector Christie wrote to my grandfather in 1943, he said, with kindly optimism – "You won't find, I think, that this dreary little time has done any harm whatsoever to a quite 'irrepressible person'. My father remained an irrepressible person, but not one who was unharmed. I think most ex-POWs might agree that to be a prisoner for any length of time exacts its toll and leaves its traces. It should be added that to be an officer POW of the Germans was, relatively speaking, an acceptable form of duress in comparison to the excruciating experience of Japanese POW camps or the ultimate and incomparable horror of the concentration camps.

I became aware of the effect of five years of prison on my father very early on in my life, as I was born not so long after the war, in 1949. Roger was then forty years old, and I was the first of three children. It was still the period of the aftermath of war – I can remember food rationing ending – and the war and its effects were, unsurprisingly, a not infrequent subject for discussion among grown-ups. Even then, my infant ears were flapping with curiosity. In my happy, rural childhood, I couldn't believe such a dreadful thing had befallen people.

My father read endless histories and biographies of both the First and Second World War, perhaps with a need to understand the full history of a period in which he had been obliged to play a long but frustrating role.

When he is in prison, a man may sustain himself with thoughts and dreams of the pleasures of home; but the reverse can also apply, that when he is a free man again, he may be haunted by thoughts and dreams of captivity, an underlying fear of it ever happening again. I know that this was the case with my father. Until the end of his life, he had nightmares about once again finding himself in prison.

> "Whether you lived eight men to a room in partitioned huts or ninety men to a cold stone barn, this remoteness of the outside world was the conditioning factor of prison life. Variations in standards of treatment and comfort made little difference relative to the permanence of this one condition."
> (*A Crowd is not Company* by Robert Kee)

In February 1943, Roger pencilled a cheerful postcard to his cousin Tom:

> "Many thanks for your letter, Captain. I'm taking life pretty easy this year – and am doing a certain amount of work in place of the abortive energies of the last two. I line up for an 'advanced German' examination in June. I am quoted with the 33-1 'Others' and expect to fail with dignified ease. Actually, I think I should fail in the 'Preliminary' but the 'Advanced' sounds so much better."

Just when everyone must have hoped that some kind of Spring was round the corner, snow fell on Eichstatt in April 1943. To his father:

> "Very cold and unpleasant here with snow. It must be wretched for John without proper clothes. I've been having one of my customary periods of rest and solitude and am embarking on another tomorrow. I find a few days of silence and meditation extremely beneficial. Please thank Guy Stanford for very kindly writing to me. I must say I always give a fairly hollow laugh when I get letters saying I'll be home soon; I've been getting them for 3 years now. It is greatly to your credit that you have never indulged in nonsense like that. I've just finished *Haig* by Duff Cooper; what a dreary individual he must have been in spite of his very admirable qualities; I've also re-read Spear's book *Prelude to Victory* – far the best war book I've ever read. I wish I could get hold of *Liaison.* Could you

10. My father (right) looking very youthful despite it all, on the day he married my mother in 1947. His best man was his friend and cousin, Tom Blackwell (left), always known as 'The Jowler'.

please send me a pair of brown corduroy trousers: they are allowed here and I think the Red Cross have at last admitted that. Many thanks for the cigarettes which arrive very steadily. Poor Alan Shearer has been very poorly – nerves I think – but is getting better. I shouldn't mention it to his father if you meet him. I think most of us have aged a good deal these three years – anyway, I got a nasty shock looking at some photographs taken in 1940. I find my eyes get very tired now, I suppose due to continual reading in indifferent light. Very many thanks for yours and Mummy's letters and attentions and best love to you both, and to all at Norcott. I can't believe its three-and-half years since I saw you last. It doesn't seem like that. Roger."

With luck, those trousers wouldn't meet the fate of the first pair, when the legs were chopped off by the Germans. What did corduroy have against it?

In the early summer, Roger had some sad news from home. He wrote to his father in June 1943:

"I can't tell you how very sorry I was to hear that *Uncle had died. I'm so very sorry for them all at

---

* Uncle Geoffrey, my grandmother's brother, was the grandson of Thomas Blackwell co-founder of Cross and Blackwell, which had been established in 1829 with a capital of £2,080. By 1892, when Uncle Geoffrey was ten, the company was worth £800,070. I have been told that

100

Norcott, they've had so much to bear this war. I'm very sorry for you too, at losing such a very old friend. I shall miss him terribly. He was always so amazingly kind and tolerant to me, and visits to Haresfoot and Norcott have formed so much of the best days of my life. I'm afraid it will be wretched for poor old John, cooped up in prison. I've written to Sophie but couldn't think of much to say. I hope she doesn't take Anthony's death too hard. Please thank Guy Stanford for another very kind letter. Your racing news is invaluable and goes round the camp at astounding speed. Here is a bit of news for Tom or anyone in my unit. Someone has just arrived here who had met Gussy Tatham and Phil Kindersley in Italy. He said they were in good heart and were the life and soul of their prison and kept the place going. He was full of admiration for Tatham whom he said he done extraordinarily well: he is recovering from wounds in the shoulder and stomach. he must be pretty old, as I was up to him at Eton when I was 14. I'm feeling rather depressed what with sad news from England, the seemingly endless prospect of captivity, and various other worries. Love to all, Roger."

---

furniture and pictures. He was married to Shirley Lawson-Johnson and had five children including John and Tom Blackwell, who were not regular soldiers, but had joined up with the Coldstream Guards at the outbreak of war.

My poor father was clearly preoccupied with troubles at this time, exacerbated by the loss of a beloved uncle, and the surfacing of memories of home.

What his particular worries of that moment were, I don't of course know, unless he had some pre-knowledge of the changes which would shortly affect him and to which he refers in his next letter. But my father always tended to be very anxious about his health, normally expressing his concern with mordant wit. His letters have often referred to the ageing process of prison. God knows, long term POWs must have felt dismally old sometimes; the feeling of impotence of being cut off from any action, the sense of youth passing in such a futile way.

Some cheering up was badly needed, and it may have been a sudden feeling of To Hell With It All, that led Roger and John Surtees to have the brief pleasure of secretly listening to the 1943 Derby, over the air waves on the Canary, the use of which was strictly confined to news broadcasts only. Who could blame them? But John says very correctly now, "This was something that should not have happened, and I don't think its use was abused at any other time." I believe the slight disaster was that one of the Canary's valves failed immediately after this brief indulgence.

This next letter, though, represents to me the nadir of my father's imprisonment. In this case, one of the causes is absolutely clear. This letter was written to my grandfather ten days later, on 30th June, 1943:

"This has been a wretched month. Today, to crown everything, most of my room have been moved to another camp, including Freddy Corfield whom I've lived with for over three years in quiet content and a considerable amount of laughter. What sanity I still possess is largely due to him. I feel very lonely and adrift now. Friendship is about the only anchor one has in prison, and now after three years I feel just as if I was starting all over again. I suppose my resistance to the bleakness of things is decreasing, but at present I feel like attaching my old school braces to the lamp bracket, fitting a snug knot behind my ears and jumping off the table. It was very kind of Uncle to leave me £100. Re the debt, he very kindly offered to square me up in November '37 before I went to Egypt, and circumstances being as they were then, I accepted his extremely generous offer. I can't really think of anything coherent to say, I'm too depressed and angry. Many thanks for the very nice Feb. clothes parcel which has just arrived. Give my best love to Mummy and Joan. I expect things will seem better soon and perhaps I'll be home one day soon. Anyway, it might so easily be worse. Roger."

Despite it all, my father gamely tries to end his letter on an encouraging note for his family at home. But Fred's departure meant more than separation from a valued friend with whom so much had been shared; it also meant the end of a very harmonious working partnership running the Canary – and if it was a job that had helped to maintain his sanity, it was one that also imposed considerable strains at times – recording and relaying the news daily – sometimes more than one bulletin in day, in constant fear of discovery of the radio by the Germans, a burden shared with the trusted Fred. The thought of continuing without him depressed him enormously, but he did continue, as broadcaster, until very nearly the end of the war. He must have had assistance, but from whom I do not know.

This seems to have been a low point for many POWs; once morale sinks below a certain point and depression sets in, it is like a virus which spreads, all those who come in contact with it run the risk of catching it. This card of 9th August is so typical of my father's response to human disaster:

> "I can really think of nothing to say which would even cover a post card. Letters have been few and far between recently. Two inmates made unsuccessful attempts to commit suicide last week – presumably from sheer boredom and despondency. I must say though, to fail even at suicide shows a deplorable lack of skill and determination. For myself, I'm bored but by no means despondent. Roger."

To his father, 20th August, 1943:

> "I wish you hadn't suggested my learning chartered accountancy this winter: it may be useful but it is hideously dull. I'm still hankering after law, especially as I can get a competent tutor. I hear you've been looking for a house in the country – how very exciting for you. I only wish I could be there too. Mummy writes very despondently as if

she had already assumed the onerous duties of sole cook and housemaid – I take that to be merely an instance of that astonishing capacity for looking on the bleakest side of every prospect which is such a feature of our family life and which I myself share to the full. Ever since I can remember we've always been hovering on the edge of a bed sitting room in the Cromwell Road, but by tremendous good fortune, we never quite seem to get there. I am quite prepared to be told that you are going up to the city in clogs, as you are unable to stump up for a new pair of prinkers. Never mind, with the money I've saved the last three years I'm quite a capitalist and will doubtless be able to assist in hiring a girl to come in once or twice a week to help with the heavy work. Of course I should like to stay in the army if possible, but if that isn't on, I should like something to do with the executive side of racing, or the police. How about the racecourse police? I'm also prepared for a small fee to succeed Bob Lyle on *The Times*. Best love Roger."

If my well-intentioned grandfather had thought to cheer Roger up by suggesting he studied chartered-accountancy, he had failed utterly!

As far as my father's future was concerned, the rest, as they say, is history. Roger left the army in 1947, submitted his first racing article, which was accepted, and in that same year, commenced work for both the *Racehorse* and *The Sunday Times*. Racing was the subject that Roger was able to study in depth as a prisoner, and many of his letters contain a reference to racing books or racing news. His talent for writing was never put forward as a plan for his future and now I wonder, if it had not been for the war, if the racing world would have ever had Roger Mortimer, racing correspondent and historian of the Turf. One thing I am certain of, there would never have been Roger Mortimer, chartered accountant.

As regards the finances of my father's family, my grandfather, as a stockbroker, was bound to be affected by the vicissitudes of the economy, both in war and peace. My grandmother, being one of the numerous children of Mr Blackwell of Cross and Blackwell, was not totally without means. But that there were anxieties about money, real or imagined, was clearly the case. My father was insecure about money for most of his life, regardless of circumstances.

But when we were young, my father had moods of sudden delightful generosity – coming home with surprise presents for my mother and for all of us (perhaps after a successful bet...) and they were always good presents, from the best shops. One of his favourites was Simpson's in the Strand. I remember the very classy Easter Eggs he used to buy us. Another great treat was the holiday book box – a selection of books for all of us, carefully chosen by him to keep us quiet occasionally on our family holidays in Brittany. We were not allowed to see the books till we had crossed the Channel, and we were rarely disappointed by his choice. From the book box, my brother developed a passion for Sherlock Holmes and 'Great Murders of the Century' and I remember happily progressing from things like *Cherry Marshall, Nurse* to Daphne du Maurier's *Frenchman's Creek* and *Jamaica Inn*. I don't recall any sexy blockbusters, but it was easier to get hold of those at school!

A September postcard suggested that Roger was back on form again:

> "Very many thanks for Abdullah cigarettes, which are excellent, and for the following books, *Letters of Princess Luvin – Long Division – Dragon's Teeth – Strip Tease Murder – Horizon Stories*. All very much appreciated. Lovely weather and lots of cricket here – some of it really high class considering the conditions – matting wicket, bumpy outfield etc., but it's been great fun. The garden's a bit over, bar sunflowers and lots of zinias. Love Roger."

Then on 21st September, a day in the life of a POW:

> "I really can't think of anything new or interesting so I'll endeavour to describe my routine at present. I usually get up with extreme reluctance at 8.30, shave, have a cold shower, make my bed and clean my shoes by 9. O'clock, when we have morning appell. At 9.15 we have breakfast in our room – a cup of tea without sugar, and two slices of bread with butter on one and jam and margarine on the other. After breakfast, the room orderly – Pte Gillespie – assisted by whoever is on duty for the room – sweeps up and washes up. I usually work in the silence room at the other end of the camp and squat on a wooden stool peering vaguely at my German

primer till 12 noon. Lunch is a plate of vegetable soup followed by biscuit and cheese. In the afternoon, I sit and read outside if it's fine, or on my bed if it's wet. Actually, I invariably do more talking and mobbing than reading. Tea at 4 p.m., the same as breakfast. Afterwards I usually walk, have a net, or take some form of exercise and a cold shower at 6 p.m. followed by appell at 6.30. Dinner at 8, the big meal of the day, meat (Red +) and potatoes followed by stewed fruit or a savoury (all Red +) and a cup of cocoa. 8.30 – 10 everyone talks their heads off and 10.30 lights out. One's room is one's castle. Other prisoners don't ever come in unless asked, and after a year, you probably don't know half the people in the next room by name. Roger."

I was somehow under the impression that prisoners confined together must know each other and be on name terms, but it turns out that as in every other society, there is a hierarchy and a code of etiquette to be observed. Francis Reed remembers Roger visiting his room at Eichstatt – obviously by invitation:

"I was in a room of sixteen (eight of whom were Etonian which the rest of us managed to survive). We were mostly in our twenties and some were only nineteen when captured. Roger was in a room of six in the same building and was a very frequent visitor to 'The Nursery' as we were known. He was about ten years older than most of us. He had done a stint with his regiment in Palestine and had considerable experience of high (and sometimes low) life in London, altogether a man of the world. How we delighted in hearing his stories.

If I seem to be making Roger out to be rather a Wodehousian character, he certainly wasn't. He was very well read and with a personal memory which must have stood him in very good stead as the famous racing journalist he became. It was said that of the 100 boys at his prep school in his final year, he could still reel off the names and numbers of ninety-eight of them."

14th October 1943, to his father:

"In my next clothing parcel, could you please send a sponge, nail brush, twenty-four Gilette blades, a pair (or two pairs) of gym shoes, some large coloured cotton handkerchiefs (for the neck), if possible a pair of suede shoes with flat rubber soles, two flannel shirts (not khaki) with attached collars, and if room, a pair of khaki drill trousers. Lovely room here. I am wearing a nice heather mixture tie knitted for me by Francis Reed out of an old sock. Roger."

Equally, Francis Reed remembers that Roger, "given a pair of home-made knitting needles and a few balls of wool, could knock up a vast sweater in about 24 hours." My father had a wonderful gardening jumper, brown heather mixture, with unexpectedly lurid cuffs in lime green and pink. He had made this as a POW from a mixture of old socks; after many years service in the garden at home, this item of woolly, war-time memorabilia took on a further life in my sister Louise's wardrobe.

Another Christmas over, and a Boxing Day letter to his father 1943:

"Very glad to get two letters from you this week – the first for over five weeks. I also got the Sept. clothing parcel, for which many thanks. I'm afraid the June one is lost, so if you could possibly repeat the contents in a later one, I'd be very grateful. Cigarettes have been very sticky lately – they came through very well in October, but I've only had one lot since. I expect they will all come through in a rush. I have received a communication from the Royal Society of Arts, informing me that I passed both intermediate and advanced papers in my examination, getting a first class in the former and a second class in the latter. The only satisfaction I can derive is that perhaps my brain is not quite as addled as you might expect. I also received the printed diplomas which might be hung up in the W.C. I'm glad to hear you're both settled in the flat, I expect you're both glad of a change. I spent a quiet Christmas yesterday – breakfast at 10 a.m. and a quiet dinner in the evening. Frankly I would have given a good deal of money for a bottle of Kummel. Best wishes to you and Mummy for the New Year and many thanks. Roger."

1943: The War Elsewhere

January: The Germans surrender at Stalingrad; 160,000 German soldiers have been killed in this long battle. 90,000 German prisoners are marched on foot to Siberia and most of those who do not die on the way die in prison. Tripoli, the last city held by Mussolini's African Empire, is captured by the Allies.

February: The US win the six month battle against the Japanese for Guadalcanal.

March: The RAF increase their bombing campaign on Germany, dropping 900 tons of bombs on Berlin and devastating Essen in the Ruhr, the industrial centre of the country.

April: Rommel evacuates his troops from Tunis after a final offensive by the Allies.

May: The Allies enter Tunis to wild acclaim. The Germans and Italians surrender in Africa. The Allies take 150,000 prisoners. The Allies bomb Sicily and a State of Emergency is declared in Italy as fears of an Allied invasion grows. The Dambusters blow up two huge German dams releasing flood tides which cause death and destruction on an unparalleled scale down the Ruhr and Elder valleys.

June: In the Atlantic, the number of ships sunk by U boat attacks has dropped considerably this year. After bombing continuously for two weeks, the Allies conquer the island of Pantelleria, an Axis stronghold between Tunisia and Sicily.

July: The Allies land on Sicily, capturing the capital, Palermo. General Eisenhower describes the victory as 'The first page in the story of the liberation of the European Continent.' The US Air Force bomb Rome. Mussolini falls from power. In Russia, the greatest tank battle in history, lasting nine days, is fought at Kurak.

August: The RAF and US Air Force bomb Hamburg solidly for a week. Shipyards and factories are reduced to rubble and an estimated 200,000 people are killed. In Italy, the Allies take Messina and bomb Rome, Turin and Milan. The Russian army advances into the Ukraine.

September: The Italians surrender unconditionally to the Allies. Battles are fought against the Germans for Salerno, Naples and Brindisi. The Russians enter Kiev, capital of the Ukraine.

October: In the Atlantic, renewed U boat attacks sink several ships. Corsica is captured by the French Resistance, the first department of France to be liberated. In the Arctic, the Allies, in the new midget submarines, place charges on the keel of the *Tirpitz*, disabling her. In Sweden, 4,200 Allied prisoners are exchanged for German ones, the first major exchange of the war. In Italy, in reprisal for their change of allegiance, tens of thousands of Italian soldiers have been crammed into sealed trucks and taken to Germany as slave labour. Italian units join up with Tito's Yugoslavian partisans.

The Germans deport thousands of Allied POWs from Italy.

November: Of the 700 U boats destroyed in the war, sixty have been sunk in the past three months. In the Pacific, the Gilbert Islands fall to the Allies. After another relentless RAF bombing campaign on Berlin, Bomber Harris declares Berlin will be bombed "until the heart of Germany ceases to beat".

December: The Royal Navy sinks the last great ship of the German Navy, *The Scharnhorst.*

*

The Beveridge Report when it came out provoked as much animated discussion among British forces serving abroad, as it did at home. It was a radical and much needed plan for the future, to make free health care and an old age pension available to everyone, through National Insurance – the conception of the now much maligned and abused Welfare State. At the time, it promised a quality of life previously undreamed of by many Britons. Roger includes his opinion in his letter to his father on 10th February, 1944.

> **"Snow is falling hard which I dislike intensely, as my bed is under the window and I'm apt to wake up and find a drift on my top blanket. Will you please thank Guy Stanford for his very great kindness in**

continuing to write to me. We have been having a number of lectures and debates on social reform and the Beveridge Plan: most people here are pretty progressive except one or two hide-bound landowners and a few *R.C.s. I think many of the reforms are long overdue and to oppose them would be short-sighted and ungenerous, and perhaps a cause of serious trouble. Certainly the Conservative party will almost cease to exist if it continues to show such half-hearted enthusiasm for what is a general and reasonable demand. Whether our economic position will be able to stand it is a very different matter. I hope Mummy's cooking continues to knock spots off Mrs. Tanner. Best love to all, Roger."

For most of her life, my grandmother had a cook, but I believe she proved to be an excellent natural cook in her own right when she was compelled to take over her kitchen. She also did some canteen cooking as a form of war work.

Guy Stanford, mentioned so frequently, was clearly a most kind and loyal friend and letter-writer. I wish I knew more about this thoughtful person.

It's with a sense of relief that I find the next letter is April 1944, because I know – which my father didn't – that he was in his final year of prison, one more Christmas, one more winter, and then liberation. It would be taking things too far to say there is a feeling of Spring about his letter, but it is certainly a buoyant

---

* Roman Catholics

11. Anthony Bamfylde top row, centre and Francis Reed top row, right.

one:

"I'm feeling horribly smug tonight wearing a new shirt and a new pair of shoes from my clothing parcel. I really am extremely grateful to yours and Mummy's efforts. I enclose a dreary little photograph – when we saw it, we all said Thank God we don't really look as awful as that – of course, in actual fact we do. It's a remarkably accurate representation, and is merely a further reminder that the truth is frequently painful to our self-esteem. By the way, do send me any photographs, and could you ask Zara Strutt to send me one of herself and godchild, and if possible, one of her wedding. To return to this unsavoury group, from left to right: the moth-eaten scarecrow propped up against the wall

12. Left to right: Fitz Fletcher, Michael Price, Phil Denison, Freddie Burnaby-Atkins, John Surtees.

wearing a self-made cap is your middle-aged and decaying offspring; John Milburn, Northumberland Hussars; Charlie 'Boots' Rome, a very old prison friend; 'Rosa' Armytage (60th or 60 7 11) who was at Wixenford with me and looks like a female groom at a sea-side riding school, but is actually a publisher and pseudo aesthete; Tony Philipson, Scots Guards,

13. From top, left to right: J. Leicester Warren, 'Boots' Rome, A. Phillipson; second row: A. Saunderson, H. Freeman Jackson, John Milburn, W. (Rosa?) Armytage, I. Weston-Smith; bottom row: Freddie Burnaby-Atkins, John Surtees, Harold Wigginston.

fresh from Italy; Harold Wigginston, a new prisoner and still just a noisy, good-natured, dirty lower boy; Francis Reed, R.B., an old prison friend, always smooth, disillusioned, acid and amusing, and lastly, wearing a pate cosy to conceal his baldness, John Surtees, R.B., an old friend (from Littlestone). After you've looked at it, shaken your head and sighed, could you send it to Hester Loyd[1] to have a laugh at. Charlie Rome had a letter from Betty Harker saying you looked thirty-five. Well I look sixty-four, so balance is adjusted. Best Love, Roger."

Needless to say, I don't have this photograph, but the photographs on pages 115, 116 and 117 feature several of the characters described, including three other dear friends of Roger's: Fitz Fletcher, Anthony Bamfylde, and Freddie Burnaby-Atkins, of whom more later.

1. Hester Loyd (later Hester Knight) had a brother, John, who was a very great friend of my father's. During the war, John died from tuberculosis, which was as the result of the wound he received at the Battle of Knightsbridge, in the desert. Two marvellous letters, which Hester wrote to my father in prison at the time of her brother's death, surfaced in his file of POW letters. As Roger cleared old correspondence from his desk with military regularity, it is just luck that these letters survived.

John and Roger had a tremendous amount of fun together before the war. Hester said that she was very much in the position of the admiring younger sister of her brother and his friends. Her letters to Roger are an example of the brave words that probably characterised all too many letters crossing the war zones of the world at that time.

> "I needn't tell you how desolate this world seems at the moment, or how empty everything is. It's only self pity that makes me weep, and John himself would understand – but I know he will be furious if we don't enjoy things and laugh just as we always have done, so that he can join in. Dear Paul – thank you for being one of his very greatest friends and for appreciating him as

you did. Don't be sad for him or for us, or for the shortness of his life, for it was so complete and so unspoilt. he was never disappointed or unhappy."

In her second letter, two months later:

"I often can't believe it's all true, and that all the things we'd planned to do once this bloody old war was over can never happen now – I know too that if it wasn't for the thought of how furious that attitude would make him, I'd be tempted to pack in and not try a yard any more, but I suppose it is just because he was such a completely exceptional person that he's managed to leave us so much of his good sense and courage (well – that does sound a trifle conceited, but you know what I mean) so as to laugh off all the dreary and stupid things – including ourselves – instead of being got down by them. Once one has got used to that time-honoured sentence 'Nothing can ever be the same again', one can start afresh and it is surprising how easy it is to do that, as long as one doesn't let oneself look back too much; the good past doesn't mix too well with either the indifferent present or the problematical future, just now, although I know that eventually it will all fall into the right perspective."

*

By September, it was understood that the end of the war, if not in sight, was not so far around the corner. Life had a point to it again. The disappointments and tragedy of both the Battle of Arnhem at the end of the month, and in December, the Battle of the Bulge in the Ardennes, were yet to come. (See notes, The War Elsewhere.) Jack Poole wrote, "All except professional pessimists had been convinced they would be home by Christmas." Unfortunately, the professional pessimists were right.

> "Year after year, abnormal influences jostled with the normal and all were considered normal. Sometimes rain lashed the tarred roofs of the huts until they glistened like the skin of a seal. Sometimes all life seemed stilled in the aquarium silence of a July sun. Always, outside the wire, the bored guards relieved each other at two hourly intervals while, inside, prisoners did the washing up or quarrelled or went to sleep. And always, inside and outside, people dreamed of the end of the war."
>
> (*A Crowd is not Company* by Robert Kee)

There was a new hint of lightness in Roger's letters:
10th September 1944:

> "Well, I'm settling down for the fifth winter in gaol, not with any noticeable degree of pleasure, but with as good a grace as is permitted by my surly and melancholic nature. Many thanks to all kind persons who wrote and assured me 'Home by Christmas' (same for the third or even fourth year running). May they not have to do it many times more. I've taken on the job of chief of the wood pile again and

am looking forward to smashing up about 200 tons of gnarled old roots. My policy is to decentralise as far as possible – in fact to do all the talking and very little of the work – a typical camp jack-in-the-office. In the evenings I half cook for the room. I'm beginning to get a sort of touch or flair after weeks of painful experimenting and I'm capable of dishing out really good stuff. There is very, very little that cannot be improvised from a basis of biscuit crumbs and a lump of margarine. At present my specialities are fishcakes, fried currant pudding and I'm coming on at 'shapes', trifle, bubble and squeak, and mock macaroni cheese. In the spare time left over I shall knit feverishly. Best Love to you all. Roger."

As the winter progressed, the reality was that communications in Germany were in a state of chaos, Red Cross parcels started to dry up and half rations became the order of the day.

To his father, 10th November:

"A very dreary day with sleet and snow driving across from the west. It's hard work on the wood pile these days as my clothes never seem to get dry and we can't afford a fire in the evening yet. A lot of clothing parcels have come in recently, mostly sent off in June, July or August, but so far, my luck is out. I'm getting very ragged in the trouser line but I've still got Tony Rolt's Sandhurst knickers which are standing the strain well. Underclothes are truly hideous and I'm continually putting my feet through the wrong hole. However, by knitting, sewing and swopping I get along alright and it's wonderful how the poor help each other. Someone told me Cecil Fielden had been wounded yesterday. I hope not badly. Cooking is rather dull on half a parcel a week and I try and save on that, as they've completely ceased to come through and we're out on Dec 15th. Altogether, this winter is rather bleak, but we all remain cheerful and try to get over shortages by ingenuity. Best Love Roger."

Peter Black was co-chef with Roger for their hut. But Jack Poole did not present quite such an enthusiastic picture of the gastronomic delights served in their hut as Chef Roger describes in his letters. But the inventiveness of these inexperienced cooks was fully challenged by the lack of almost any ingredients to cook with. Jack wrote:

"A representative example of dinner at this stage was meat muck-up followed by bread pudding. Meat muck-up consisted of half a tin of bully beef between six men, mashed up with some indifferent turnips and potatoes supplied by the Germans. Bread pudding was devised from old bread crusts soaked in water, 'gingered up' with a few raisins, prunes and figs, then baked."

Peter Black recalled: "To be a cook for your mess meant quite a lot of power. You had complete control over the food stocks and could dictate what was to be consumed and what was to be saved (mossed up – as we called it) for a rainy day. Also it meant that one did not have to wash up or help clean the room. In the course of time we were inevitably deposed by our companions and I forget who took over. (We left for our successors a magnificent oven, which an Australian had constructed for us out of stolen bricks – *sic transit gloria mundi.*)

"Your father and I must have cooked some very indigestable meals there. Between us we nearly did for poor Jack Poole, who woke up in the middle of one night with a burst duodenal ulcer. We managed to alert a guard – quite a feat in itself, as they were apt to shoot first and ask afterwards."

Jack was bound to have a more detailed and painful memory of this incident, and he recorded it:

"One freezing December night, I awoke in acute pain and complained of my discomfort to my room mates. Roger's immediate assessment of my condition was 'A very nasty attack of wind', the inevitable consequence of dinner. But it was quickly realised that I urgently needed a doctor. To walk the four hundred yards from the hut to the hospital block would have certainly meant coming under fire from at least two sentry boxes. The only solution was to alert the attention of the nearest sentry and explain the situation.

The window was opened wide, the bitter night air streamed in, and Roger began a series of plaintive cries in indifferent German to attract the sentries' attention. The nearest sentry, unfortunately, was not in that keen state of alertness he should have been. In fact it was strongly suspected he was dossing down in a corner of his elevated box, as it was a long time before the cries of 'Ullo, Posten' received any answer at all. When at last he did reply, he gave an exhibition of obstinate stupidity that drove us all nearly insane. He refused to communicate with the guard-room, and pretended he could not comprehend what all the fuss was about. In the meantime, I was in dire agony, and the yellers at the window were being rapidly frozen. After what seemed a full hour, but was probably not more than fifteen minutes, the big oaf sulkily rang up the guard room."

Before the night was out, Jack was removed by car to the Roman Catholic hospital near the camp, where he was operated on by a good German military surgeon, and nursed with care by the nuns there.

*

Roger sent his "Christmas letter" off to his family on 10th December, 1944:

"Best Wishes to you all for Christmas and the New Year, and if you get the chance, could you remember me to Guy Stanford, Lily, Mrs. Tanner, Nanny and Barrett. It is snowing hard here which is better than the endless rain we'd been having. After three months of saving, I hoarded enough to make a pretty big Christmas pudding – breadcrumbs, margarine, raisins, apricots, prunes, sugar, beer, marmalade, egg powder, a tinned apple pudding and biscuit crumbs. I wrapped it up in greased lavatory paper, tied it up in Everard's towel and steamed it madly for 7 hours. It is now hanging up from a hook on the wall. The flat sounds nice, but I pity you moving. I know something about moves and they're

'Surely not Sauerkraut in Christmas pudding, old boy.'

By Gordon Horner.

hell. No sign of any clothes or food parcels, or I fear, those cigars you kindly sent. I had a record week on the wood pile last week and we cut up about 9 tons with three saws and three axes on spite of stinking weather. It doesn't seem like five years since I saw you all, and as far as I'm concerned, absence only makes the heart grow fonder and I don't mean that in the ironical sense. Roger."

I am totally impressed by my father's Christmas pudding. I have been told that as he had no currants, he chopped up a black shoe lace and added that for good measure – apparently nobody noticed the difference!

1944: The War Elsewhere

January: In Italy, thousands of British and US troops land at Anzio. The Russian army smashes through the German lines which have kept Leningrad besieged for two years. Russian troops cross the pre-war Soviet border into Poland. Eisenhower becomes Supreme Commander of Allied Invasion Forces in Europe. In the Far East, the Allies launch an assault on the Marshall Islands. Three escaped US officers have made statements describing the brutal conditions in Japanese POW camps. Thousands of American POWs have died on marches to prison camps in the Philippines.

February and March: In Russia, a two week battle on the Ukrainian front leaves ten divisions of the German 8th Army destroyed. The Allies successfully attack a number of Japanese positions in the Pacific. In Burma, an Allied force, and equipment, are dropped 200 miles behind Japanese lines and within twelve hours, had carved out an airstrip in the jungle for a fully equipped fighter squadron. In Italy, the Allies bomb the monastery at Monte Casino, which had become an impregnable German fortress, then launch a major assault on the area. The US Air Force launches 'Operation Argument', a week of continuous bombing of German aircraft factories and port installations. In Hungary, Adolf Eichmann, responsible for the deportation of Jews to Auschwitz, arrives in Budapest.

April: The Russians open their campaign in the Crimea and begin the Battle of Sebastapol. For Hitler's fifty-fifth birthday, the Allies carry out the biggest single bombing raid, simultaneously attacking areas of Germany, France and Belgium. US Forces land on New Guinea. General de Gaulle becomes Commander in Chief of the Free French Forces. Britain makes its final preparations for the Allied Invasion of Europe.

May: Stalin directs Bulgaria, Rumania and Hungary to declare war on Germany. The Russian army captures Sebastapol. British and Polish forces capture Casino. Allied forces breaking out of Anzio link up with the 5th Army. A single Allied front now stretches across Italy. Fifty British and Allied airmen recaptured after tunnelling their way out of an 'escape proof' prison camp in Silesia, are shot.

June: Rome falls to the Allies. D-Day, the Allied Invasion of Europe, the biggest combined air, land and sea operation of all time. Conducted successfully and in spite of appalling weather conditions and being under continuous bombardment, and though suffering many losses, the Allied troops land in Normandy.

Following the strategy of heavy bombing in Germany, the same approach is being employed to destroy the Japanese war industry. Hitler's secret weapon, the jet propelled, pilotless, buzzing bombs, the V1s or doodlebugs, which are designed to explode on impact, strike at Britain.

July: After over a month of fighting in Normandy, the Allies take Caen. The battle for Normandy becomes the battle for France. In the first Free French Invasion of France, forces land between Nice and Marseilles. In Britain, two and a half thousand deaths have been caused by doodlebug attacks. Soviet troops attack Warsaw.

The July Plot – an assassination attempt on Hitler fails.

August: The Allies enter Paris. The German Commander von Cholitz defies Hitler's order to destroy Paris before surrendering. General de Gaulle declares "I wish simply and from the bottom of my heart to say 'Vivre Paris'." Rumania signs an armistice with Russia and declares war on Germany. Collaborators in the plot to kill Hitler are hung by piano wires strung from meat hooks. The Warsaw Uprising begins.

September: Allied troops liberate Belgium to scenes of near delirium in the streets of Brussels. Allied Forces break through the major defence of the Siegfried line. Nancy, the key German bastion in eastern France, is liberated. V2 rocket warheads, faster than doodlebugs and also soundless, attack London.

The Battle of Arnhem, a dramatic airborne operation

which promised to bring the end of the war much closer, ends tragically. After a week of battling against a combination of impossible odds, the British pull back across the Rhine. Of the original force of 10,000, only 2,400 return.

October: British troops land in Crete. After three and a half years of German occupation, a small group of Allied soldiers and a band of Greek partisans enter Athens to ecstatic greetings. In Yugoslavia, Belgrade is liberated by Soviet troops and Tito's partisans. Aachen becomes the first German city to fall to the Allies. The Japanese suffer their most crushing defeat so far in the Battle of Leyte Gulf in the Philippines. Polish Home Army surrenders in Warsaw after Soviet help is cyncially withheld by Stalin.

November: Soviet tanks enter Budapest. Germany's last major warship, the *Tirpitz*, is sunk. The British Home Guard is put into retirement. Lights are switched on in Piccadilly for the first time after five years of black-out.

December: General Patten's troops reach the Siegfried line. The beginning of the Battle of the Bulge, where twenty-four German divisions launch a major attack on the unprepared Allied force of 80,000 in the Ardennes. In a final flying bomb attack on England on Christmas Eve, the rockets also contain letters from British POWs which scatter in pieces of confetti when the bombs explode.

*

To his father, New Year's Day, 1945:

> "Well, here we are at the beginning of another dreary year of prison life; it is increasingly hard to visualise liberty. Prison has ceased to be an episode and has become one's normal life. One's pre-war friends are vague memories, and one's friends are those of your fellow convicts that you can still tolerate after living at close quarters with them for four-and-a-half years. Naturally, we get duller and more useless year by year and I think our worst feature is that we are all very great bores indeed, self-centred, critical, and altogether dim. One's existence in the winter is entirely based on food and fuel and it certainly hasn't been a gala winter for either. Books never arrive, or at any rate, very rarely, and one's correspondents dwindle away year by year. If anyone write to me this year and assures me I shall be home for Christmas, I shall regard it as a very bad omen indeed. I hope prison life will become more normal during the coming year and books, clothes, cigarettes will start filtering through again. An officer from Nigel Baker's company has turned up here; he was at his private school when the war started. Well, best wishes and love to you all for the new year. Roger."

My father made many of his closest and lifelong friends during his internment, but as he has frequently pointed out, very few human relationships can be maintained at their best, year in, year out, in such testing circumstances. By January 1945, the middle of another hellish winter, they must have all had enough.

Francis Read said, "Those last months of the war were trying ones. There was the dread uncertainty (not always expressed) as to what the defeated Nazis would do with a lot of useless POWs. If asked what kept us going in those dreary days, I would say chiefly laughter. Roger's great friend, Jack Poole, prefaced his autobiography with those lovely words of Hilaire Belloc's:

> *"From quiet homes and first beginning,*
> *Out to the undiscovered ends,*
> *There's nothing worth the wear of winning,*
> *But laughter and the love of friends."*

Roger Mortimer supplied a lot of the laughter for which many of us are eternally grateful."

THE CLOSING MONTHS

The atmosphere at Eichstatt for the last few months of the war was characterised by mood swings of the greatest hope and elation to deepest gloom and despondency. Rumours abounded on the nature of events and the way in which the war would be concluded – one story would quickly be eclipsed by another, and at one minute the prospect of home seemed only weeks away and at another, months – or worse, that the final debacle might involve death and destruction on some scale.

New prisoners, or those being transferred from other camps, were still being brought into Eichstatt regularly and of course, they were fresh sources of information on the movements of the Allies, the intentions of the Enemy, and which camps were likely to be moved on as the Germans retreated.

So there was much speculation on the form the liberation would take. Jack Poole wrote:

> "There were several schools of thought: those who assumed somewhat naively that the Germans would hand us over in good order; others who knew (very Hush Hush, this) that special squads of paratroopers were standing by to drop on all those camps and guard us until friendly armies arrived; and those who didn't care, so long as no mental or physical exertion was required by them. Roger Mortimer, who never suffered wind-bags gladly, added this comment: 'Well, if you ask

me, we'll be lucky not to be carved up like a Bank Holiday ham.'"

As things turned out, in April 1945, my father's prophecy fell not wide of the mark, although what was to occur, and the nature of the event, had not been a part of his prediction.

*

If there were any remaining letters from Roger in 1945, they would surely have conveyed some of the atmosphere of those uncertain times, but they would not have been able to reveal day to day developments. It would have taken a diary or journal to do that, a form of record that was discouraged if not entirely forbidden to POWs. I have been very fortunate in being given access to the 1945 prison diary kept by Desmond Parkinson which paints a picture of those last months – emotions oscillating between optimism and despair, between anticipation and trepidation, and sometimes, an underlying anxiety on how it would feel to return home again.

For the next few pages, the story becomes more personal to Desmond than to my father, but at the same time, the views they held, and the feelings they experienced as POWs, rather than as distinctly different individuals, probably had much in common. But there is an immediacy about Desmond's diary, a youthfulness, a feeling of the here and now, that gives one a sense of

14. Desmond Parkinson.

journeying with him through those unsettling days building up to liberation. He wrote with a candour unrestrained by the responsibility of reassuring loved ones at home.

Extracts from: 'A DIARY FOR 1945' by Lt. D.F. Parkinson, POW No. 636, No. 2 Company, Oflag VIIB, Eichstatt

"I am convinced that during 1945 our captivity will end. Therefore it is likely to be a year on which I shall always look back for the rest of my life. For this reason – undaunted by many past failures – I am embarking on this diary in an effort to record for my own personal interest the impressions and emotions which I experience.

Very probably, when the war nears its end, I shall be so excited and out of control that sitting down each day to make an entry in this book will simply be out of the question.

Monday 1st January. Thanks to a German edict to the effect that the store of Red Cross parcels was to be rapidly reduced, for once we were not short of food. Since it is New Year's Day, Parade was not until 9.30. This was followed by an enormous breakfast of porridge, eggs, sausages, toast, butter, marmalade and coffee.

1945 has started off pretty well, but, nevertheless, I am dreading a return to the world of gloom and hunger through which I have been passing recently. Rumours of repatriation are thick upon the ground and it is difficult not to be a little excited. Oh how wonderful it will be to return home, as I've absolutely had this existence and everything to do with it.

Thursday 4th January. For various reasons, I haven't continued this great work until now. Since last writing, I have felt very depressed. What I am lacking completely is peace of mind and the ability to settle down. Even reading a book is beyond me. Nevertheless, I am optimistic enough to hope that in a month or so, I will return to normal once more. My sense of humour tells me that if and when I read this diary after the war, this particular entry will seem unbelievable and even laughable.

On Tuesday, we went to see *A Comedy of Errors* – a terrific production with excellent music and acting. Just before the end of the show, the air-raid siren sounded, with the result that, until an escort turned up, we were stranded in the theatre. When we finally got back to our room, we had to cope with dinner in the dark.

Wednesday was a terrible day as I was stooge and thus spent most of my time engaged in menial tasks. Whilst I was so engaged, John kept asking me footling and impossible questions on Spanish grammar.

For the past few days, there have been rumours of repatriation for old prisoners. Freddie and I have made a bet; if we are not home or in a neutral country by 15 March, I am to pay for a dinner party in London.

Sixty new arrivals are due to turn up here at any moment. There is great speculation as to who they will be. I always have a hope that one day someone I knew before the war will turn up.

Wednesday 10th January. In the afternoon I had to polish my shoes to prepare myself for a dinner party given by Fanny (Yes a nickname, Ed.). Contrary to my expectations, I much enjoyed this party. Everything was slap up. Roddy Mcleod was the other guest, and as I was sitting between my host and John Robertson, conversation was no problem. We started eating at 7.15 and were still going strong at 9.30 when I had to take my leave.

Monday 15th January. BLACK MONDAY
2.45 p.m. Great rumours of a search preceded today and we all went on Parade well wrapped up and ready for anything. Everyone was convinced that the search was going to be for food, as today is the end of the 'Bashing Era'. The SBO Jack Higgin addressed the Parade and announced with some well chosen comments that the Germans had decided to take some quite inhumane reprisals against us for conditions alleged to exist in a German POW camp in Egypt. As a result, all our mattresses, chairs, stools and tables are to be taken away. In addition, all public rooms are to be closed. As the SBO pointed out, there are only two of these anyhow. Thereafter, a whole mass of fully armed SS troops entered the camp, accompanied by some other odds and sods who proceeded to our rooms and got on with the job of removing all our furniture. It was the coldest morning imaginable, but in spite of everything, including the prospect of freezing discomfort every night, everyone was quite remarkably cheerful and treated it all as just another 'Cherman Choke'.

After three and a half hours, we were allowed back to the chaos of our rooms. The room looks very bare and empty, but luckily we have been left (presumably through an oversight) two rocker chairs. Thanks entirely to Freddie, who has lent me his lilo, I have managed to make my bed and it looks more comfortable than it was before, but maybe it's a lot colder. Most people have now got themselves more or less organised and are trying out their reconstructed dossers. Whatever the discomfort, these events have had the effect of raising morale considerably. This was reinforced by a visit from Dick Troughton who recounted some of the more amusing happenings of the day ... a mattress being thrown out of a window onto the head of a passing German carrying a load of stools ... the pinching and burning of a whole cart of furniture left outside block 1. In his own room, Dick had written in chalk on the floor "This is the table – keep off".

Tuesday 16th January. Thanks to the lilo, I had quite a comfortable night, but others were not so lucky. The complete lack of tables and chairs hasn't troubled me yet, but it will become a bore having either to stand up the whole time or lie flat on one's back.

Saturday 20th January. Since all concerts, music and entertainments have been banned, a plan has been born that we should form a small band which could go and perform in a different room each evening. The band is to comprise Eric Arden on a mini piano, me on the clarinet and John Davies on guitar. I only hope we don't get arrested.

Wednesday 24th January. We are now back again in very cold bleak weather. Some brave souls have built a mini ski jump on the steepest bank around. Morty (Roger) came in for a brew and was in colossal form. He talked most amusingly of his experiences at Sandhurst and as a subaltern.

Saturday 27th January. Got out my old Sandhurst boots and put them on in preparation for a day's outing with the wood-party next week. Freddie was out (wood collecting) yesterday and returned exhausted, after a really cold day, just in time to do the cooking for John Surtees's birthday bash. In the afternoon I had to unload the wood trailer – hard work but I got beautifully warm. I then went for a long walk with Fitz Fletcher. He really is an excellent companion and nothing seems to ruffle him.

Monday 29th January. In the evening *Morty came to visit us and was given stick by one and all.

Saturday 3rd February. This was easily one of the best days I've spent in captivity. I was woken up soon after seven and had a big struggle putting on my boots and Morty's puttees in the dark. Freddie, John, Fitz, Charlie, Wiggie, Harry and I formed the party from this room. We left the camp at 8 am and it was just our luck that Freddie and I were picked out by the guards and taken off to be body searched – an event which, thanks to Morty, was public throughout the camp within ten minutes.

We then set off in the trailer and travelled out via the Castle and junction. It was all great fun, but my feet got very cold until I was warmed up later by loading wood onto the trailer. This task was completed by 11 am, when we made our way to the hut with cocoa and bread etc. There was little serious work done for

---

*   Morty = Good old Roger Mortimer!

the rest of the day and I shall always remember the feeling of peace, and impression of feeling free once more.

Monday 5th February. A wonderful spring-like morning and I woke up feeling that all was well with the world.

Thursday 8th February. A lovely day today but the fine weather has made me feel very homesick. I got slowly more depressed until the early afternoon, when Everard came in and dragged me out for a walk. In the evening, our "clandestine" concert party gave its first performance. It was fun to do and we got an excellent reception.

Sunday 11th February. In the course of a walk with Freddie, we solemnly discussed the effect of five years in captivity upon us. We concluded we had not suffered much but had learnt an awful lot about other people.

Tuesday 13th February. The highlight of the day was a most interesting lecture entitled 'From D-Day to Arnhem' given by one of the new arrivals. It filled us all with tremendous optimism for the future.

Wednesday 14th February. A big air-raid during the night with planes coming in very low. Again at midday, the sirens sounded once more, so I spent the afternoon reading and writing a p.c. to Mum. Since I have had no letters, writing is no easy task.

Thursday 22nd February. Freddie, Fitz and I left the camp at 8 am and were detailed to cut up wood.

This kept us very busy all day. The high spot was an air-raid when American fighters came zooming just above us and then shot up the junction.

Saturday 24th February. Out with the wood party again today. We saw hundreds of American bombers coming over fairly low and dropping incendiaries. A wonderful sight.

Monday 26th February. Yesterday was a wonderfully restful day. There was another air raid alert and Charlie Rome claimed that he had counted 346 bombers.

Tuesday 27th February. In the morning, a recently captured RAF officer called on us and gave a fascinating talk on the latest bombing techniques. As soon as he had finished, the alarm sounded and the air raid went on until 4 p.m. These raids are becoming a bore, as far as we are concerned, as it means that we have to spend the best part of every day indoors. To make matters worse, food is now once again in very short supply and I am hungry.

'*I say, can you tell me where one collects food — I'm a new Kriegie.*'

By Gordon Horner.

Wednesday 28th February. More air raid alarms. Great optimism is in the air and I have not yet written off my 15 March bet with Freddie. Everyone is now making up address books and knocking up packs and other containers in preparation for the journey home. There is a most disquieting air of restless excitement. In the evening went down to Hut Room 2 to give another performance but had hardly got started when, for the third time in the day, the alarm went so we had to pack it in.

Thursday 1st March. The beginning of another month... maybe this is the last? If not, we are in for a lot of hardship, as food and cigarettes are practically non-existent. Once more confined to our rooms by air-raids.

Friday 2nd March. Soon after 11 the inevitable siren sounded. Luckily, our soup somehow got through the blockade. Am becoming more and more hungry.

Saturday 3rd March. Today the weather stood proxy for the RAF. It snowed all day and it was too foul to venture out. Morty came in for a brew and we talked about the news and current events. Everyone is now very optimistic because of the good news from the West, and I find myself thinking more and more of home as the end comes nearer. Later in the day, Freddie and I had an animated discussion about pork pies and chocolates. It is terrible to find one's thoughts constantly turning to food again, but so far I have not been uncomfortably hungry.

Sunday 4th March. Last night our small band entertained the orderlies. They gave us a great reception

Freddie Burnaby-Atkin's Prison Identification Card, 1940.

and, moreover, we were treated to a cup of real army cocoa. I am very depressed today for no apparent reason. These bouts seem to be fairly commonplace among us five year 'Kriegies' and are usually triggered by something quite insignificant. With me, these moods never last long and I am recovering now as I write this.

Friday 9th March. Terrific optimism abounds today. My own was helped along by a hot wash and much better weather. Inevitably, this brought with it another air raid alarm. I was later able to go out for a walk with John who is in excellent form again. I also had a walk with Charlie, who, ever the optimist, is firmly convinced that another six weeks will see the end of what he calls 'this dreary business'. Most people seem to agree with him. Parcels came up at tea time – a mixture of French, Belgian, American and Canadian. I scoffed my ration of chocolate in double quick time. It was a great change having some meat for supper again. It gave me a lot of extra puff for our subsequent concert in Block 3.

Saturday 10th March. The weather is back again to its dreary form and partly due to this, there is a terrific feeling of anti-climax throughout the camp. Most people are at a pretty low ebb just now. We all agreed that unless more parcels arrive very soon, we are going to be extremely hungry, especially since it has been announced that all our German rations are to be cut by one fifth.

Sunday 11th March. Played with the band in Ian's room. I must admit I am getting very tired of these concert parties.

Wednesday 14th March. We were kept on parade until 11 am while the Germans once more took away our mattresses – mine included. A really gorgeous spring day and luckily there has been no air raid to spoil it. The real excitement has been the arrival of 3,000 British Red Cross parcels.

Friday 16th March. So I have lost my bet with Freddie about the date of our repatriation. Nevertheless, I am very much looking forward to giving him that dinner. Spring is really here and I am bursting with energy.

Sunday 18th March. Tonight, we organised a Brains Trust party in our room. The panel consisted of a Dutchman, a Belgian, a Frenchman and a Greek. The Dutchman was the star of the show, especially on the subject of atrocities.

Tuesday 20th March. Sat outside with Steve and Morty until the air raid alarm sounded at midday. The news seems wonderfully good and there is a great air of excitement. Spent the evening reading until Morty and Charlie descended on me for a gossip.

Thursday 22nd March. 8,000 Red Cross parcels have arrived. We shall still be on a ration of half a parcel a week, but the bogey of starvation has been given a nasty knock.

Friday 23rd March. There are rumours that the British have crossed the Rhine in the north.

Tuesday 27th March. It appears from the German

papers that the rumours of the Rhine crossings are true. This has caused great excitement.

Wednesday 28th March. The highlight of the day was an issue of a tin of condensed milk per head and 2oz bar of chocolate. I downed all of mine in ten minutes with the greatest of ease. Marvellous. Rumours still abound. The French are said to have broken through in the south. But, more serious from our point of view, there are allegedly 1,000 officers on their way from Oflag Va. The camp is already overcrowded and that will mean our previous food supplies will be cut by a third.

Thursday 29th March. Late in the evening, two Red Cross lorries, with 1,600 parcels aboard, turned up. They were driven by two Canadians on parole. They had some fantastic rumours... riots in Berlin and Munich... parachutists at Stuttgart... allied tanks at Ulm and Augsburg, etc. The war really does look as though it must end soon, but whereas two days ago I was expecting to see American tanks at any minute, I am now relatively calm.

Friday 30th March. The main story is that the Yanks are in Stuttgart. What is for sure is that five thousand truck loads of food have arrived. As a result, we shall be on a full parcel a week again.

Saturday 31st March. As each day brings us nearer to the end of the war, I find that stress gets greater and I pass from exhilaration to depression and vice versa, with lightening rapidity and for no apparent cause.

Charlie and Morty came and talked to me, the latter very gloomy and predicted that we would have a summer of foot slogging from camp to camp. There is a compound at Moosberg labelled 'Eichstatt' and we were very nearly moved there last Monday. I'd give anything to stay here peacefully until the end.

1st April. Easter Sunday. A great day and a wonderful beginning to what really must be our last month in captivity. I got up early and went to communion with Charlie, and then returned for a terrific breakfast of porridge, meat-roll, bacon, potato, toast, butter, jam, marmalade and tea. Terrific. I gave Fitz some tooth powder as a birthday present. Later I went to Church with Freddie; I enjoyed letting myself go in the hymns.

Monday 2nd April. In the interest of my fitness campaign, I did three circuits of the camp.

Tuesday 3rd April. Terrific rumours are about today and once more I am getting very excited. The wood party saw refugees from Rottenburg, which has been occupied by the Americans, and the word Ausbach is on every lip tonight since it is only 40 miles from here. Eisenhower and Kesselring are said to be discussing peace terms... if we move we will have to go across country... the commandant is packing... the Armistice will be signed on Wednesday... there are three deserters from the Guard Company... Eichstatt is to be defended etc. etc.

If all these stories are true, in the next few days we will either be liberated or we will be foot slogging across Germany. Colonel Thompson has decreed a general tightening up of discipline and we now have to salute senior officers and appear on morning parade washed and shaved. There is a big outcry for the issue of more food.

Wednesday 4th April. Jack Poole came to see us in the morning and was in excellent form. He was followed by an American Officer, Col. Alger, who recently marched across Germany; he gave us a rather gruesome account of his adventures. Shades of things to come perhaps?

Friday 6th April. We now have breakfast every morning and this extra food makes a tremendous difference. I then had an extra bonus in the shape of seven letters. All of them were over three months old.

Saturday 7th April. There is a most uneasy atmosphere of panic, as every other minute a new rumour reaches our room. It is almost impossible to relax. Because of this I did no less than ten circuits of the camp – four with Freddie and six with Phil Denison. The latter has a very direct way of expressing himself and I find his company very refreshing.

This evening we saw thousands and thousands of prisoners on the march. This has made me want to stay here more than ever.

Monday 9th April. Glorious weather. I was able to spend the afternoon lying in the sun with Charlie and Morty.

The story of the day is that during the night a German orderly woke up the Commandant with the news that the "Americans are here." He was referring to three American prisoners, but the Commandant immediately panicked and burnt all his papers!

At tea time there was an air raid and we counted 510 bombers and 45 fighters. Not a German plane in sight. It is also said that the British Government has announced if the Germans move British POWs around, they will retaliate in the same way on German prisoners.

Friday 13th April. We are now definitely to move to Moosberg on foot on Saturday morning.

Saturday 14th April. BLACK SATURDAY.
The most tragic, terrifying and emotional day of my life – anyway as a prisoner.

This was the day of the great march. It started at 6 am when we had a large breakfast of porridge and tea. By 7 o'clock, we were down on the parade ground with all our kit. Mine is much too heavy as it weighs something like 80lbs, of which some 30lbs must be food. I have also 1,500 cigarettes. There was a wonderful array of home made carts, knapsacks, etc. and everyone was in marvellous form. By the time we moved off from the camp at 8.30, I was exhausted, but John, Freddie and I helped along by dint of laughing at ourselves and other people, managed to go about a mile to the first halting place, where we took off our packs and relaxed.

At about 9.30 we saw a solitary plane in the sky. It flew over our column several times and we saw that it was an American fighter. A great cheer went up from all of us. The plane circled round us several times and then waggled its wings and flew off. This all served to raise our morale a good deal, but some twenty minutes later, eight Thunderbolts appeared on the scene, and to our surprise, started bombing and strafing a convoy of lorries on a parallel road some 800 yards across the valley. The general reaction was that the reconnaissance plane had recognised us and had

149

called up the fighters to put on a show for our benefit. Personally, I didn't share this view because I thought it was all too close for comfort. After dealing effectively with the lorries, all eight planes then swept down on to our column which was spread all over the road; we were all gawping upwards and were totally unprepared for the tragic disaster which was to follow.

As the first plane came over, it opened fire and all the others followed suit. Again and again the planes swept down and strafed us from practically road level. Mercifully, they must have used up all their bombs on the lorries.

By this time, Freddie, John, Morty and I were trying to make ourselves as small and inconspicuous as possible in a little hollow some ten yards off the road. We felt horribly exposed and very frightened. My first instincts were of self-preservation, but this soon gave way to complete fatalism, punctuated by prayers and thoughts of my family.

There was a lull after ten minutes which seemed more like an age. We shifted our cover to the wall of a nearby house where we felt a little more secure. By this time, a Union Jack had been spread across the road and when the fighters returned, they did not open fire. This was just as well, as our casualties were being tended.

At last, we were told that we could make our way back to the camp, or go to the woods. Our small party decided on the former course and we set off across the fields beside a river, carrying our absurdly heavy kit. I have never been so thankful to get back anywhere as I was to reach the comparative sanctuary of our camp.

As we came down the strasse, bits of news were already flying around. We heard that Phil Denison had been hit. It later transpired that overall casualties were eight killed and forty-two wounded. To my mind this was a miraculously small total considering how exposed and helpless we were.

I must admit that this whole episode has shaken me badly, like most other people too. The fact is that after five years of this unreal life, one's powers of resistance to any shock are practically nil and all the terror and tragedy of the morning has hit me deeply. The worst part of it is that I now have very little faith that it won't happen again. I would do anything to avoid a repetition. Luckily, we are to spend the night here and march off at dusk tomorrow evening, only moving at night. This will give us all a chance to regain our balance.

I thank God that all my own friends are safe and sound. Poor Freddie has not been so lucky as we heard this evening that Humphrey Marriott has died from his wounds. This is all very hard to bear, but from Humphrey's point of view, I feel that his death has been a merciful release, since such an energetic and cheerful chap would have hated to go on living as a cripple. Rosie (Walter Armytage) tells me that Phil is not yet out of danger but they hope he will be O.K. Eric Arden has lost an arm, and Johnnie Cousins a leg.

I spent the rest of the day repacking my kit, thinking non-stop about the morning's events and being terrified of any aeroplane I saw or heard. Even here we do not feel very safe and large POW signs have been painted all over the camp. it is depressing to think that, before the day of our liberation, the line of battle will have to pass over us and that today's horrors may only be a foretaste of things to come."

*

One day when I was young, I went for a walk with my father, and something of the scenery we strolled through must have reminded him of that Spring day in Germany so long ago, that Black Saturday. He told me his memory of that devastating event as we walked. The story had a great effect on me. It was certainly the first time I appreciated that in war, through incompetence or accident, and sometimes through strategic necessity, it was possible to die at the hand of your friends as well as your enemies. I was very shocked by that.

Reading Desmond's account, written in the fresh and raw immediacy of the event, sent a chill through me. I found it additionally poignant that although they both lived to tell the tale, my father and Desmond might have died beside each other in that air attack. Forty-six years later, when my father's life drew to a close, Desmond was at his bedside, with my mother, at the moment of his death.

*

The next day, 15th April, those fit enough to do so, although worn and tired, set off, in sections, to march by night (as a precaution against air raids) to Moosberg in Lower Bavaria, not far from Munich. Most were carrying heavy loads – all their kit including, as Desmond said earlier, quantities of food, for the future was uncertain, and conditions at Moosberg were said to be dire.

The first stretch of the march ended at 4 a.m. Desmond, John and Freddie were billeted in the barns of a friendly farm. As they lay down to rest, "cocks were in full cry – a noise I hadn't heard for the best part of five years," wrote Desmond.

At 9 p.m. that evening, they set out on the march again. The Germans had told them it would be an 18 kilometre walk, but it turned out to be thirty, before footsore and utterly exhausted, they reached their next resting point. After marching so long in darkness without light, colour, view, or warmth from the sun to cheer them along, it must have been difficult not to lose heart.

On 17th April, the news came through that *Phil Denison had died. "This is a great blow to all of us," wrote Desmond.

On 18th April, Desmond, and Freddie, who was afflicted with a number of problems including raging toothache, were billeted at a farm where they were able to sleep and wash, and where they found the native villagers very friendly. They learnt that American patrols were reported to have crossed the bridge over the Da-

---

* Phil Denison was the brother of my godmother, Sonia Heathcote-Amery.

15. On the left Martin Gilliat and on the right Freddie Burnaby-Atkins after the war, in New Delhi. Later, Fredddie became the Comptroller of Princess Margaret's household, and Martin was Private Secretary to the Queen Mother.

nube that the POWs had crossed two nights previously.

In Desmond's diary, there is a sense of pleasure in the good things of life seeping gradually back, "I would very much like to spend the rest of the war on one of these farms. Today we have seen a foal, calves, piglets, kids, goslings and baby chicks. We sadly took our leave of the village at 9 p.m. to start the next stage of our journey."

It took another four days marching to get to Moosberg, during that time, spirits were rising as the prospect of liberation came closer and closer.

In the gallant British officer style that prevailed regardless of circumstances, Desmond and Freddie found themselves being "invited to dinner" one evening, "A terrific spread of fish soufflé, bacon and eggs, M & V bake, oatcakes, beer and tea. I staggered back to bed feeling really full. Shortly after we settled down, Freddie announced that he was feeling sick and then promptly upchucked all over the straw. A furious voice from below shouted "Upstairs there – is anyone doing a pee up there?"

In contrast, that same day, "A large column of British troops passed through the village. They had been on the move since January and were in a very poor way as they had to subsist solely on meagre German rations. I can't yet imagine the frightfulness of such a march in really cold weather. We have been really lucky, but even now it is hard enough to keep warm at night, and once wet, you just have to stay that way. These men had several casualties from frostbite. There were no officers with the column, and no medical personnel."

In his diary entry of Monday 30th April, Desmond confessed to enjoying the march, for all its discomforts: "After the dull monotony of camp life, it was marvellous to lead a pseudo Gypsy existence and to enjoy comparative freedom. All the way, people were amazingly friendly."

At 10 a.m. on that day – a very cold one – they marched through the gates of Moosberg Camp. They had reached the end of one journey, and the start of the final one that was to take them to England, and home.

1945: The Final Months

January: The Germans have been under intense attack by Allied bombers in the Battle of the Bulge. Troops and supply lines have been pulverised and the Germans are being squeezed out of the Ardennes with heavy losses. The city of Warsaw finally falls to Soviet troops. Hungary declares war on Germany. Auschwitz is captured by Russian troops. The remaining 5,000 inmates are found on the brink of death from starvation and disease.

February: U.S. troops break through the Siegfried Line. 6,000 Allied bombers attack German transport lines and in the most controversial Allied bombing of the war, the RAF and US bomb Dresden, leaving it a smoking ruin with 130,000 people killed. The Allies close in on a continuously bombed Berlin. 500 POWs are freed in the Philippines after US troops advance twenty-five miles in Japanese-held territory.

March: The Allied Armies cross the Rhine. Churchill, visiting the 21st Army Group along the Rhine, wrote in Montgomery's autograph book on March 26th, "The Rhine and all its fortress lines lie behind the 21st Group of Armies. A beaten army not long ago Master of Europe retreats before its pursuers. The goal is not long to be denied to those who have come so far and fought so well under proud and faithful leadership. Forward on all wings of flame to final Victory."

THE DARKNESS BEFORE THE DAWN: MOOSBERG (Stalag VII A)

Peter Black was with Roger at Moosberg, their final camp, which as predicted, turned out to be quite the worst prison of the lot. Things were not helped by the mood of the Germans, who, of course knew they had lost the war and it was only a matter of time before surrender. Germany was in chaos and this was certainly reflected by conditions in a camp where there was one tap per 400 people, no facilities for cooking at all, nothing to do, nowhere to sit or lie down during the day, and the perpetual, filthy stench from an overburdened sewage system. Mercifully, it was to be the darkness that comes just before the dawn.

Peter Black has written this chilling description:

> "Moosberg had a grim, carved wooden entrance, engraved, presumably by prisoners, with the words 'Abandon hope all ye who enter here', and adorned with carved figures of people in the depths of misery and despair. Not a very attractive welcome.
>
> There were, I think, about 45,000 prisoners in this camp, of every conceivable nationality. Things had more or less broken down by the time we arrived and it was a case of 'sauve qui peut'. There were starvation rations of a sort. I think we lived on what we had saved from Red Cross parcels. There was a lot of disease and it could be quite dangerous to stroll about the camp by yourself. You could stray into a bad area and get set upon. Everything had collapsed at that

stage, except the guards with rifles pointed at you.

The *Russians were particularly badly treated, and if you threw one a cigarette, it was most likely that his companions would scrag him to death for it. They mainly looked like large or small Kruschevs. There were very few Metropolitan-looking Russians. They wore many wrist watches on both arms right up to their shoulders. I don't known where they got them. The watches must have been currency for them. I think these people were mostly shot when they returned to Russia.

In the event of the Russian Army reaching us before the American troops, which at that time was quite likely, your father had arranged to escape with a Coldstream Guards' Sergeant, who had laid on some papers and a different uniform. I escaped once on the way to Moosberg, but was recaptured by the Germans. I would certainly have tried to avoid falling into the hands of the Russians.

---

* "Strangely enough the most cheerful people in Moosberg were the Russians. Pre-war, too many Russian films had given me the mistaken idea that Ivan Ivanovitch was a gloomy soul, but the Russian soldiers I met were full of fun, even when their bellies were empty – and they were certainly tough. Jerry, who continually used large police dogs for 'smartening up' purposes, was foolish enough to let one run wild in the Russian compound at night. A couple of Ruskeys had it for dinner and in the morning, Jerry was proffered the skin – all that was left." (From *For You the War is Over* by Gordon Horner)

Among the prisoners at Moosberg were quite a lot of American officers, mostly pilots; Indian officers; Poles; Czechs; even Greeks, in addition to the ordinary troops. Guarding the perimeter, there was a company of Waffen SS who, when the Americans approached the camp, shot up the ordinary German guards who wished to surrender. When the Americans entered the camp, a group of prisoners – Russians I think – chopped down one of the wooden watch towers with German soldiers in it and tore them to pieces when they fell to the ground.

So, we had quite a little battle over the camp. I remember diving under a hut until things quietened down, as there was no point in losing one's life in those circumstances. Everything subsided when Patten entered the camp in his jeep, complete with his pearl-handled revolvers. I don't think he lingered.

At the very end, we got onto a good racket with some US officers and administered the whole camp. A sort of idiotic *coup d'etat*; the only good racket I ever got onto."

The camp fell on 29th April.

Mess Sergeant, Bill Graham, Coldstream Guards, who was a great fan of my father's, was standing beside him as the American Sherwood tanks rolled through Moosberg – "An American sergeant, whose brother was on the relieving force, gave me to bottles of Martel brandy, one of which I gave to your husband," he wrote to my mother, in the nicest letter, after my father's death in 1991.

Prisoners were issued with United States Government V-MAIL forms. The instructions proclaimed "V-Mail service provides a most rapid means of communication". It was the nearest thing to a telegram. "V-Mail letters may be sent free of postage by members of the Armed Forces." On his V-Mail form, my father wrote the following:

> "I was 'liberated' on Sunday, but God only knows when I'll get back. I've been walking across Germany previously and having a good time on the whole. This camp is the end – the absolute end – filthy, indescribable squalor; 400 per hut and one tap for cooking, washing, etc. and thousands in tents with no water at all. It is absolutely beyond description. It is nice being without Germans after five years. They were unutterably mean, treacherous and oppressive from first to last. Thank God they're getting a Hell of a pasting. I saw General Patten some days ago. I've over-eaten the last few days and now feel extremely ill – most people are in the same condition. I've seen lost of German prisoners passing including some very mean SS types. I can't say how much I'm looking forward to seeing you all again. Best Love, Roger."

The pent up rage of five years' misery exploded on to the single page allowed for rapid communication.

I leave the last few days to Peter Black:

> "Eventually we wandered off to an airfield at Landschat, which was under constant sniper fire and this

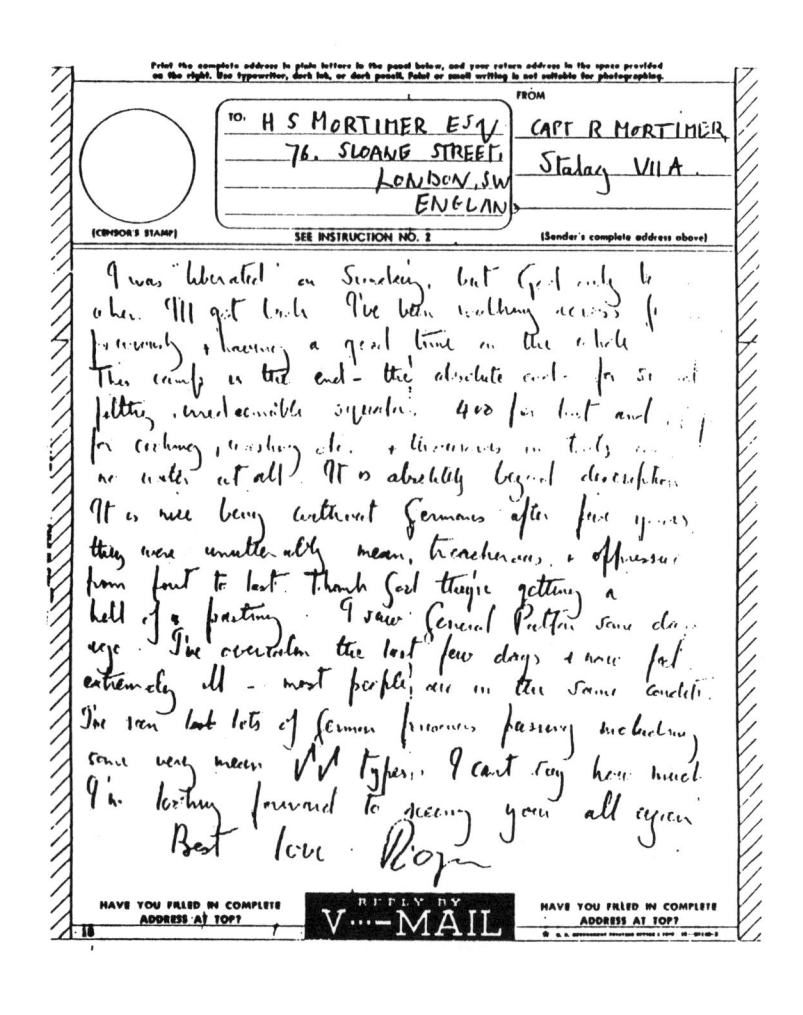

My Father's 'Liberation' letter.

caused a lot of the aircraft to land badly and occasionally collide with each other. Your father and I turned out a family in a house on the edge of the airport, sleeping there at night and in the morning, walking to the airfield where we would spend the day hoping to get on one of the aircraft. There was some sort of order and organisation but everything was hit or miss.

The roads were choked with refugees and D.P.s (displaced persons) of every description: men and women in their twenties, looking sixty or seventy years old.

We were flown back to England by a Canadian Bomber Squadron. Roger and I were separated at this juncture. I remember that Fitz Fletcher and I were in the same aircraft, in some very uncomfortable part of the aeroplane, but I don't think we minded about that."

My Aunt Joan had a friend in the WRNs whose brother, Bobby Wheeler, was also in prison with Roger. Roger had made a point of searching him out and liked him a lot. Bobby had been in the same party as my father on the walk to the aerodrome at Landschat. On the morning of departure, they were allocated to different planes. Bobby's plane hit a pylon and everyone in it was killed. That these men had suffered enough, for long enough, gave them no immunity from final tragedy when they had been but within hours of home. My father did not learn of this sad news until he was back in London.

*

Who can measure time? There are days which flash by in a minute, and hours which drag like year. Time is subjective. When my father put his feet down on English soil again in May 1945, did he feel that a lifetime had passed since he went away? So often in his letters home he had said, "It doesn't feel like so many years since I saw you all."

When my father entered the airport building, he found that a kind committee of local ladies had laid on a great spread of refreshments to welcome the returning POWs. But he just couldn't face it. He was too shocked and disorientated.

My father's first step back to normality was going to the Gents, where he retired with a fresh copy of one of his great pleasures in life – *The Times*. Two very ordinary aspects of civilisation, a proper W.C. and a daily newspaper were his first two steps back to a normal life.

1945: The End of the War

April: Bergen, Buchenwald and Dachau are liberated. Mussolini and his mistress are shot by Italian partisans and strung up by their heels in front of a petrol station in Milan. Twenty-two German Divisions and Italian Fascist Divisions surrender unconditionally to General Alexander at Casserta. Hitler, whom Churchill had described as a "bloodythirsty guttersnipe" in 1940, shot himself in his bunker. Thirty out of seventy POW camps of Allied Prisoners are liberated.

May: The final and complete surrender of all German forces.

May 8th: VICTORY IN EUROPE DAY.

THE AFTERMATH

After the War, my father often met up with his POW comrades in London. When they had been compelled to be together, many must have been the moments that they wished to be apart. And now that they were, there was, my father said, a need to be together again as they re-adjusted to their own lives in a country which had also changed. They were united by a shared experience which they had no need to explain to each other.

They also had a great deal of catching up to do. Roger, John Surtees, Desmond and Freddie Burnaby-Atkins saw a lot of each other in London, and I can imagine they were quite a foursome – handsome, intelligent and fun and ready to let their hair down – as Freddie said, "We sowed a great many wild oats pent up from five years incarceration."

Today, the process of adjusting to a POW experience would be supported, undoubtedly, by psychiatric consultation and endless forms of therapy and counselling. Then, there was nothing. Ex POWs might have been described as suffering from Post Traumatic Stress Disorder, or similar term but they just had to get on and make the best of things. It was up to each individual to find his own way of coming to terms with the shadow of the recent past.

Outwardly, lives moved on. Inwardly, the experience of being a Prisoner of War left an indelible mark. All future experiences and relationships were to some extent coloured by it. There are many ex POWs still living for whom the experience is still too painful for recollection or discussion.

To have come through the dangers of war alive was in itself a form of great good fortune and a cause for gratitude, but it could not completely eliminate the punishing effects on a man of being deprived of a number of the most potentially vigorous and productive years of his life, in such a seemingly pointless manner. The futility of imprisonment was deeply demoralising.

Fred Corfield wrote that he became involved with politics in the fifties, "basically because I wanted to make up for being so useless to the country as a POW". That he had done the best he could – the Canary bird, for one example – to continue to function as an officer of the British Army, in the most frustrating and restrictive of long term circumstances, was surely an honourable contribution.

To have endured, to have tried, to have lost neither heart nor hope, nor humour, nor human values – that is a courage of its own order. To have been a Prisoner of War was not to "Have had a good war". It was to have had a bad war which demanded any number of 'good' qualities to survive it.

My father did not harbour any long term hatred for the Germans, recognising that they too, had ultimately been the victims of Nazism. In the 1950s, my parents employed two German au pair girls, good old Ingrid and Valtraut. Later, my parents took several holidays in Germany, mainly in the Black Forest. On one occasion, my father took my mother to see Eichstatt.

Perhaps it is of some consolation to POW survivors that their stories continue to move us, inspiring those of us who have not experienced war directly, by their stoical example.

The Canary Bird

As far as Roger and the Canary were concerned, most of his friends were of similar view.

Fred Corfield, Roger's broadcasting partner for two and a half years, wrote: "As far as I know, there was no word of thanks to Roger, except from our news readers and those of our friends who were in the know. However, the effect on morale, has I think, been fairly widely recognised, so that this lack of recognition of our contribution at least reflects our success in enforcing secrecy."

Jack Poole: "Despite somewhat unconventional treatment, the Canary was rarely sick or sorry, but Roger told me he had to face some ugly criticism after a valve went as he was having a quiet private session listening to the 1943 Derby."

"When circumstances allowed, everyone in the camp (Eichstatt) had a full news bulletin daily, and three times a day in periods of excitement. Camp morale was greatly dependent on the contents of these bulletins, and it is impossible to exaggerate the effects of Churchill's speeches, particularly when the outlook seemed murky.

"Few of us at the time fully appreciated the unending work of our wireless team, and as the years slipped by we came to accept as routine that news would always be available at certain hours. Roger Mortimer stuck it out for four years. His faintly cynical manner as a purveyor of news masked a rational stability of a very high degree and I envied his cool nerve."

John Surtees: "Your father's great service to all the thousands of POWs was never properly recognised."

Francis Reed: "For anyone who has not experienced the dreariness of POW life, it is difficult to understand the importance we placed on receiving news from home. Of course it wasn't a solo effort and I cannot write these few lines without mentioning Roger's long time colleague and friend, Freddie Corfield. What I don't think many of us realised at the time was the tremendous strain the daily chore of listening to the Canary placed on all the participants – chiefly Roger, and many years later, sitting peacefully by the fire together, Roger spoke at great length and with much feeling about this. With no proper shorthand he yet managed to take down verbatim Churchill's speeches and in June 1944, several bulletins a day on the invasion. Roger always denied that all this ruined his handwriting for the remainder of his days.

The award of honours is a tricky subject but there must be a very large body of POWs who would have been delighted if Roger had received some official acknowledgement for his sterling work."

16. *My parents on their Wedding Day.*

A New Beginning

Within six weeks of meeting my mother, Cynthia Denison-Pender, in 1947, my father proposed to her.

My mother's war had not been uneventful. She joined the FANYs in 1939, initially working as a driver of Blood Transfusion vans in Bristol, then was transferred to the Senior Officer's College in Wiltshire. When the FANYs amalgamated with the ATS, she had two choices – to become an ATS Officer or to continue at the Senior Officer's College and 'drive randy officers round Salisbury Plain' – neither choice appealed to her. She longed to go abroad but was still under the age limit of twenty-one, for foreign service. She then did a number of jobs; looking after bombed out babies in a home in Oxfordshire, 'land girl' work on he father's farm, then to London, against her parents' wishes, to drive a mobile canteen to the docks, anti-aircraft and barrage balloon sites, returning home towards the end of '41 to work as a trainee draughtswoman at Westlands Aircraft Factory at Yeovil, where she stayed for two years before returning to London to work as an ambulance driver for the Red Cross, in the Blitz, and later transporting returning POWs, mainly from the Far East, to their homes in the London area.

In August 1945, my mother, as a Red Cross Driver, was entitled to a place on the steps of St. Paul's for a National Service of Thanksgiving. Inside the cathedral, my father was acting as an usher. They had not yet

17. The Mortimer family taken by The Sporting Life in 1965! Jane and Charlie on chair, and Louise on the stool. Also, Pongo the dalmatian.

met. Later, Roger claimed that he had spied her there.

My mother left the Red Cross in 1946 and had planned to train as a picture restorer, before my father swept her off her feet. They were married in St Paul's, Knightsbridge on 10th December, 1947.

SOME BIOGRAPHICAL DETAILS

Sir Frederick Corfield, Q.C.: Fred Corfield, under the influence of a distinguished Cambridge Law Don, Professor C.J. Hamson, took his Bar exams while in prisoner of war camp (Rottenburg), where he was sent in 1943 having been in the same camps as my father up until that point. In 1945, he married Ruth, to whom he had been engaged since February 1940. He retired from the Army and became a farmer. He gave up farming on becoming M.P. for South Gloucestershire in 1955. He then combined politics with a practice at the Bar. He held several ministerial appointments while the Conservatives were in office and was made a member of the Privy Council in 1970. He was sacked by Heath in 1972, but then given a knighthood. He retired from politics in the 1974 election and then worked full time at the Bar. He became a Q.C. in 1972 and a Recorder in 1974. He retired from both in 1982.

John Surtees: John was a 2nd Lieutenant in the 1st Battalion of the Rifle Brigade at the start of the war. The Battalion went to France in the emergency situation of May 1940. He fought in the Battle of Calais. He had arrived on 22nd May, the battle started in earnest on 23rd May and it was all over by 26th May. Nine officers of his regiment were killed and all but five of the remaining officers were wounded. John insisted that it was because of the totally dauntless performance of his officer contemporaries in the 1st Battalion – very largely those who were killed fighting against hopeless odds – that he was recommended for an M.C., which he received when he returned home in 1945. He was wounded in action and taken prisoner. His capture took place on the sand dunes of Calais on the afternoon of 26th May. After a spell in two French hospitals, he was transported to Spangenburg POW camp in Germany at the beginning of August 1940.

After the war, in 1949, John became a partner in a small firm of wine importers which later expanded considerably. In the 1960s he also joined the Government Hospitality Committee (which has built up a quite exceptional cellar) and the Royal Household Committee. He still very much enjoys being a member of both of these organisations. He also became one of the first ten Masters of Wine in 1956. He has been married twice and has two daughters. He now lives in Wiltshire.

Desmond Parkinson: Lt. Parkinson was also captured in May 1940 and initially taken to Laufen POW camp in Germany.

Immediately after the war, he served with the Army on staff jobs in Palestine, then Gibraltar. In 1949, he resigned his commission and joined the Foreign Service. He served in Rangoon from '50-'51, Morocco '57-'59, Nigeria '59-'60. He subsequently served in Singapore, Kuala Lumpur and Delhi. From 1967 he was engaged in work in London until he retired in 1975, when he was awarded the CMG. Desmond is married to Paddy and lives in Hampshire. He has four children from his previous marriages.

Francis Reed: Francis joined the army in August 1939 and received his commission with the Rifle Brigade in January 1940. He too was captured on 26th May 1940, on the beach at the Battle of Calais.

After the war, he worked in publishing from 1946 to '52. He then became involved with the antique trade until 1961 and for the next twenty-five years worked for a charity which provided aid to European refugees. In 1988 he had various heart attacks and has described himself as having slid rapidly down hill 'from a wrinkly to a crumbly'.

Peter Black: Married Monica not so long after the war. They lived in a delightful house, Cabbage Cottage, in Cheshire for many years. For some time now, they have lived in Jersey. Peter has been badly tested by his health for a number of years, but remains as charming as ever.

Jane Torday: Mother of two sons. Lives in Northumberland. Has worked as an advertising copywriter, in an art gallery, as a bookseller and as a postmistress. In the past she was an occasional contributor to national and local media. Previous publications are – *101 Presents to Cook, A Little Book of*

Old Fashioned Nursery Recipes, An Idiot's Introduction to Gardening, Looking Back – A collection of Northumbrian Childhood Memories, Wish Me Luck As You Wave Me Goodbye – Northumbrian Memories of World War II. She is currently studying Garden Design.

Charlie Mortimer: Lives in London. Charlie's job list, after a spell in the army, includes vintage car restorer, oil rig worker, estate agent, lorry driver (including a number of trips to Poland on relief missions, driving a heavy goods vehicle). For the past decade he has worked as Business Manager to the Hobbs Brothers, Antique Dealers in Pimlico. For several years he has worked regularly as a counsellor for a Self-Help group in London.

Louise Carew: Mother of a daughter and a son. Lives in London. Louise is a teacher in charge of a tribe of small boys at a school in Chelsea. She is planning to develop her interest in remedial teaching. She is also a keen traveller – something she hopes to do more of in due course.

Index

21st Army, 157
5th Army, 127
8th Army, 58, 80

Aachen, 129
Abyssinia, 55
Africa, 111
Afrika Corps, 41
Albania, 26
Alexander, General, 165
Alexandria, 10
Alger, Colonel, 148
Algeria, 25
Allan, Les, 8
Allied Invasion of Europe, 127
Allies, 80, 87, 110-111, 113, 126-129, 156
America, 68
American bomber planes, 141
American fighter planes, 141, 149
Americans, 148, 153
Anzio, 126-127
Arabs, 10
Arctic, 112
Arden, Eric, 138, 151
Ardennes, 129, 156
Armistice, 147
Armytage, Walter, 115-116, 117, 151
Arnhem, 140
Arrowe Park, 63
Ascot, 23-24

Athens, 49, 129
Atlantic, 41, 49, 111-112
Atlantic Charter, 55
ATS, 172
Auchinlek, General, 80
Augsburg, 146
Ausbach, 147
Auschwitz, 80, 126, 156
Australia, 77
Axis powers, 79

Bader, Douglas, 75
Baker, Nigel, 130
Bamfylde, Anthony, 115, 118
Barclay House, Yateley, Hampshire, 60
Barrett, 69, 124
Bataan, 80
Bath, 80
Battle of Arnhem, 128
Battle of Britain, 25
Battle of Calais, 93, 174, 176
Battle of Guadalcanal, 111
Battle of Knightsbridge, 118
Battle of Leningrad, 58
Battle of Leyte Gulf, 129
Battle of Sebastapol, 127
Battle of Stalingrad, 87, 110
Battle of the Atlantic, 26
Battle of the Bulge, 129, 156
Battle of the Midway, 80
Battle of the Somme, 14
Bavaria, 79
BBC, 74

178

Belgians, 145
Belgium, 20, 23-25, 42, 127-128
Belgrade, 129
Benghazi, 41
Bergen, 165
Berlin, 111, 113, 146, 157
Beveridge Report, 113
Birks, 69
Bismarck, 49
Black Forest, 168
Black Saturday, 149, 152
Black, Peter, 8, 76, 82, 122, 158, 161, 163, 176
Blackwell, Geoffrey, 70-71, 73, 100, 103; John, 51, 77, 98, 101; Mr, 106; Shirley, 70-71, 73, 86; Tom, 21, 51-52, 98-99, 101
Blitz, 172
Blythe, Ronald, 38
Borneo, 79
Brindisi, 112
Bristol, 172
Britain, 25, 87, 127-128
British Army, 26, 32, 40, 167
British Expeditionary Force, 15
British Forces, 35, 49, 127
British Government, 148
British Home Guard, 129
British Navy, 32
British Peace-keeping Force, 10
Brussels, 128
Buchenwald, 165
Budapest, 126, 129

Bulgaria, 41, 127
Burma, 79, 88, 126
Burnaby-Atkins, Freddie, 8, 66, 116-118, 136-137, 139-140, 142, 145, 147-9, 150-51, 153-55, 166

Caen, 128
Cafe de Paris, London, 52
Calais, 94, 175
Cambodia, 55
Cambridge, 11
Canadians, 146
Canary, The, 7, 42-44, 46, 48, 54, 59, 67, 76, 82-83, 102-103, 167, 169-170
Caserta, 165
Cazenove, Arnold, 19
Chamberlain, Neville, 24
Christie, Hector, 84, 88-89
Churchill, Winston, 24-25, 44, 55, 79, 87, 157, 165, 170
Cobbold, Ralph, 70-71
Colditz, 53
Coldstream Guards, 10, 15, 20-21, 78
Cologne, 80
Commandant of Eichstatt, 148
Compeigne, France, 25
Coombe-Tenant, Henry, 76
Corfield, Sir Frederick, 7, 29, 34, 36, 39, 42-45, 48, 50, 59, 62, 67, 75-76, 79, 83-84, 103, 167, 169-170, 174; Lady Ruth, 45, 174

Corregidor, 80
Corsica, 112
Cousins, Johnnie, 151
Coventry, 26
Crete, 49, 129
Crimea, 127
Cripps, John, 84
Cross and Blackwell, 106
Cummins, Ethel, 68, 70-71
Czechs, 160

D-Day, 127, 140
D-Day Normandy Landings, 82
D.L., 86
Dachau, 165
Damascus Gate, Jerusalem, 11
Dambusters, The, 111
Danube, 153
Davies, John, 138
de Gaulle, General, 127
Delhi, 175
Denison, Phil, 116, 148, 150-151, 153
Denison-Pender, Cynthia, 172 (see also Mortimer, Cynthia)
Denmark, 25
Derna, 41
Dieppe Raid, 81-82, 87
Dresden, 156
Dunkirk, 24, 35
Dunne, Peggy, 70-71
Dutch, 145

East Africa, 40

Egypt, 25, 80, 103, 137
Eichmann, Adolf, 126
Eichstatt, 79, 82-147, 168
Eisenhower, General, 111, 126, 147
El Alamein, 80, 82, 87
Elder valley, 111
Emily, 69
England, 101, 129
Eritrea, 41
Essen, 111
Ethiopia, 41
Eton, 14, 31-32, 101
Eton Corps Camp, Tweesledown, 31
Everard, 124, 140
Exeter, 80

Fanny, 136-137
FANYs, 172
Far East, 172
Fielden, Cecil, 121; Major Jerry, 19, 21
First World War, 14, 48, 93
Fletcher, Fitz, 66, 116, 118, 139-140, 147, 163
Fort Kingston, Canada, 46
France, 25, 35, 80, 87, 112, 127-128, 174
Freeman Jackson, H., 117
French, 32, 145-146
French Armistice, 1940, 25
French Resistance, 80, 112

Gaulle, General de, 25, 128
Geneva Convention, 51
Genoa, 87

180

Gerard, Rupert, 17-18
German 8th Army, 126
German General, 23
Germans, 8, 25-26, 35-36, 39, 42, 46, 49, 53, 55, 58, 77, 80-81, 87, 94-95, 110-112, 132, 137-138, 148, 153, 156, 167
Germany, 23, 39, 54, 65, 111-113, 121, 127-128, 147, 156, 168, 175
Gibraltar, 175
Gilbert Islands, 113
Gillespie, Private, 107
Gilliat, Martin, 154
Gilroy, Bobby, 91
Goldman, Private, 59
Gore-Brown, Tommy, 17-18
Gort, Lord Field Marshal, 35
Graham, Bill, 160
Grange Con, County Wicklow, Ireland, 21
Greece, 26
Greeks, 145, 160
Greek partisans, 129
Green Jackets, The, 84
Guinness, Posie, 21

H.M.S. *Ark Royal*, 58
H.M.S. *Hood*, 49
H.M.S. *Prince of Wales*, 58
H.M.S. *Repulse*, 58
Hamburg, 26, 112
Hampshire, 176
Hamson, Professor C.J., 174
Haresfoot, 101
Harker, Betty, 116-117

Harris, Bomber, 81, 113
Harry, 139
Hasleden, Mr, 34
Higgin, Jack, 137
Hitler, Adolf, 13, 20, 24, 36, 41, 55, 81, 127, 165
Holland, 24-25, 93
Hong Kong, 58
Hore-Belisha, Minister of War, 16
Hungary, 126-127, 156.

Imperial War Museum, 83
Indians, 160
IRA, 54
Italian Fascists, 165
Italian partisans, 165
Italians, 25, 41, 55, 111-112
Italy, 25, 87, 101, 111-112, 116, 126-127

Japan, 55, 58
Japanese, 55, 79-80, 111, 126-127, 129
Japanese POW camps, 126
Jauncey, Mr., 69
Jersey, 176
Jerusalem, 10
Jews, 10, 55, 58, 80, 88, 126
Johnson, Herbert, 64; Snake-Hip, 52
July Plot, 128

Kee, Robert, 8, 27, 62, 68, 91, 97, 120
Kesselring, General, 147
Kiev, 112
Kindersley, Phil, 101

181

Kings Own Regiment, 12
Kuala Lumpur, 175
Kurak, 112

Landschat, 161, 163
Langley, Jimmy, 59
Laufen POW camp, 94, 175
Leicester Warren, J., 117
Lemprière Robin, Raoul, 8, 20
Leningrad, 126
Libya, 25, 49
Licensed Victualler's Association, 84
Liddell, Alvar, 44
Littlestone, 116-117
London, 14, 26, 36, 49, 80, 88, 108, 128, 166, 172, 175
Louvain Canal, Belgium, 20
Low Countries, 20
Lower Bavaria, 152
Loyd, Hester, 116-118; John, 118
Ludgrove, 37
Luin Dujeproges dam, Russia, 55
Lyell, Lady Sophie, 61, 70-71, 101
Lyle, Bob, 105

Malaya, 58, 79, 88
Malta, 41, 58
Mansell, John, 36
Marriott, Humphrey, 151
Marseilles, 128
Marshall Islands, 126
Mauley, Lord Gerald de, 8
Mcleod, Roddy, 137

Mersa Matruh, 80
Messina, 112
Milan, 112, 165
Milburn, John, 115, 117
Miller, Mrs., 73
Mitchell, Chris, 21; Star, 21
Monte Casino, 126-127
Montgomery, Field Marshal, 87, 157
Moore, Philip, 61
Moosberg, 147, 152, 155, 158, 160
Morocco, 175
Mortimer family, 21; Charlie, 7, 32, 106, 173, 177; Cynthia, 7, 152, 171; Dorothy, 20-21, 37, 64, 86, 99-100, 104; Harry, 10, 21, 37, 63, 73, 77, 84-86, 93, 98, 102, 130; Jane, 6, 173, 176; Joan, 21-22, 64, 163; Louise, 7, 109, 173, 177; Roger, 1, 3, 10-11, 14-15, 18, 20-21, 23, 29-31, 34, 36-37, 40, 42-44, 46, 50-51, 59-60, 62-66, 71, 76, 78-79, 85, 94-95, 97-99, 102, 104-105, 108, 113-114, 116-118, 122-123, 130-133, 138-139, 142, 145-146, 148, 150, 158, 161-164, 166-167, 169-171
Moscow, 58, 88
Mountbatten, Lord, 81-82
Munich, 146, 152
Mussolini, 112, 165
Mussolini's African Empire,

182

Mussolini's African Empire, 110

Nanny Mabel, 37, 69, 124
Naples, 112
National Ex-Prisoner of War Association, 8
Nazis, 80, 88, 131
Nazism, 10, 167
Neave, Airey, 34, 53
Nelson, Jane, 70-71
New Guinea, 79, 127
New Zealand golf club, 72
Newark, 69
Nice, 128
Nigeria, 175
Norcott, Berkhamstead, 64, 69, 99-100
Normandy, 127
North Africa, 41, 44, 49
Northern France, 21
Northumberland Hussars, 115
Norway, 24-25
Norwich, 80

Oflags, 50; Oflag Va, 146; Oflag VI B/2 Bn, 59-81; Oflag VII B, 82-135; Oflag XI A/H, 27-41
Oxfordshire, 172

Pacific, 80, 113, 126
Palermo, 111
Palestine, 10, 108, 175
Pantelleria, 111
Paris, 17, 25, 55, 128
Parkinson, Desmond, 65, 72, 133-136, 138-140, 142, 144, 147-149, 151-153, 156, 166, 175-176
Parknson, Desmond, 7
Patten, General, 129, 160-161
Pearl Harbour, 58
Petain, Marshall, 25
Philippines, 58, 126, 129, 157
Philipson, Tony, 116
Phillipson, A., 117
Phoney war, 15
Piccadilly, 129
Pilkington, Gerry, 84, 86
Plaice, Mr, butler, 64, 69
Poland, 25, 46, 48, 50, 126
Poles, 53
Polish forces, 127
Poole, Jack, 9, 74, 91, 93-95, 120, 122-124, 131-132, 148, 169
Pope, Lance, 42
Price, Michael, 66, 116
Prittie, Terence, 84
Purdue, William, 8

RAF, 8, 32, 75, 80-81, 83, 87, 111-113, 141-142, 156
Rangoon, 175
Read, Francis, 131
Red Cross, 27, 48, 61, 66-68, 85, 99-100, 108, 121, 135, 144-146, 172
Reed, Francis, 8, 51, 62, 92, 108-109, 115-116, 170, 176
Rhine, 129, 146, 157
Rifle Brigade, 174, 176
Robertson, John, 137

183

Rolt, Tony, 84, 121
Rome, 112, 127
Rome, Charlie, 34, 115, 117, 139, 141, 144-146, 148
Rommel, Field Marshal, 41, 49, 80, 87, 111
Roosevelt, F.D., 55
Rottenburg, 147, 174
Royal Navy, 25, 113
Royal Scots, 12
Royal Society of Arts, 110
Ruhr, 111
Rumania, 26, 127-128
Russia, 54, 58, 112, 126, 128
Russian Army, 80, 112, 126-129, 156, 159
Russians, 62, 127, 159

Salerno, 112
Sandhurst, 12, 138
Saunderson, A., 117
Scharnhorst, The, 113
Scots Guards, 116
Sebastapol, 80, 127
Second World War, 20
Shape, Edward, 69
Shearer, Alan, 99-100
Siberia, 110
Sicily, 111
Sidi Barani, 26
Siegfried Line, 128-129, 156
Silesia, 127
Singapore, 175
Singapore, Fall of, 79
Solomon Islands, 79
Somaliland, 41
Somerset, Nigel, 51

Soviet army, 156
Spangenburg Castle, 27-29, 32, 40, 43, 48, 59, 175
St. Nazaire, 80
St. Paul's, London, 172
Stalags, 50-51; Stalag VII A, 158-161; Stalag XX A, 50-58;
Stalin, 55, 127
Stalingrad, 81-82
Stanford, Guy, 86, 98, 101, 113-114, 124
Strutt, Zara, 115
Stuttgart, 146
Sumatra, 79
Surtees, John, 8, 29, 32-34, 44, 46, 59, 62, 65, 82, 102, 116-117, 136, 139, 144, 149-150, 153, 166, 170, 174-175
Sweden, 112

Tanner, Mrs., 20, 69, 114, 124
Tatham, Gussy, 101
Thailand, 55
Thatcher, Mrs., 54
Thompson, 69
Thompson, Colonel, 147
Thorn, 50-59, 83
Tirpitz, The, 112, 129
Tito, 112, 129
Tobruk, 41, 49, 58, 80, 82, 87
Tojo, General, 58
Toulon, 87
Tripoli, 41, 110
Troughton, Dick, 138
Tunis, 111

184

Tunisia, 111
Turin, 112
Tweesledown, 31

U boats, 26, 41, 58, 80, 87, 111-113
U.S.S.R., 55, 80
Ukraine, 112
Ulm, 146
United Nations, Declaration of the, 79
US Air Force, 112, 126

V-Mail, 161
V1 rockets, 127; V2 rockets, 128-129
Vichy France, 25
Vichy French North Africa, 88
Victoria Station, London, 21
von Cholitz, General, 128

Warburg, 59-82
Warsaw, 128, 156
Washington, 88

Wavell, General, 44
Welfare State, 113
Welsh Guards, 76
Western Desert, 26
Westlands Aircraft Factory, 172
Weston-Smith, I., 117
Westphalia, 27, 62
Wheeler, Bobby, 163
Whitaker, Jack, 19
Wigginston, Harold, 116-117, 139
Willet, Peter, 1
Wiltshire, 172, 175
Wixenford, 37, 116
World War II, 8

Yeovil, 172
York, 80
Yugoslavia, 49, 129
Yugoslavian partisans, 112, 129

185